GREAT TRAMCARS

THE BLACKPOOL STREAMLINED TRAMS

GREAT TRAMCARS

THE BLACKPOOL STREAMLINED TRAMS

PETER WALLER

Pen & Sword
TRANSPORT

AN IMPRINT OF PEN & SWORD BOOKS LTD.
YORKSHIRE – PHILADELPHIA

The Blackpool Streamlined Trams

First published in Great Britain in 2020 by
Pen & Sword Transport
An imprint of Pen & Sword Books Ltd
Yorkshire - Philadelphia

Copyright © Peter Waller, 2020
© Photographs: As credited

ISBN 978 1 52670 904 2

The right of Peter Waller to be identified as Author of this work has been asserted by him in accordance with the Copyright, Designs and Patents Act 1988.

A CIP catalogue record for this book is available from the British Library.

All rights reserved. No part of this book may be reproduced or transmitted in any form or by any means, electronic or mechanical including photocopying, recording or by any information storage and retrieval system, without permission from the Publisher in writing.

Typeset in 11/13 Palatino by SJmagic DESIGN SERVICES, India.

Printed and bound in India by Replika Press Pvt. Ltd.

Pen & Sword Books Ltd incorporates the Imprints of Pen & Sword Books Archaeology, Atlas, Aviation, Battleground, Discovery, Family History, History, Maritime, Military, Naval, Politics, Railways, Select, Transport, True Crime, Fiction, Frontline Books, Leo Cooper, Praetorian Press, Seaforth Publishing, Wharncliffe and White Owl.

For a complete list of Pen & Sword titles please contact

PEN & SWORD BOOKS LIMITED
47 Church Street, Barnsley, South Yorkshire, S70 2AS, England
E-mail: enquiries@pen-and-sword.co.uk
Website: www.pen-and-sword.co.uk

or

PEN AND SWORD BOOKS
1950 Lawrence Rd, Havertown, PA 19083, USA
E-mail: Uspen-and-sword@casematepublishers.com
Website: www.penandswordbooks.com

CONTENTS

Abbreviations 6
Acknowledgements 7

The Early Years 8
The Post-War Years 17
The Franklin Era 34
The Years of Retrenchment 46
Into the 1970s 68
The End of the OMO Cars and Developments through to the Millennium......100
Into the Modern Age 128
Illuminated Trams 139
Preservation 145

Appendices 146
Bibliography 151

ABBREVIATIONS

BTH	British Thomson-Houston Co Ltd	M&T	Maley & Taunton
CP	Crompton Parkinson	MCW	Metropolitan-Cammell-Weymann Ltd, Washwood Heath, Birmingham
EATM	East Anglian Transport Museum, Carlton Colville	NTM	National Tramway Museum
EE	English Electric	SEPTA	Southeastern Pennsylvania Transportation Authority
GEC	General Electric Company		
LRTA	Light Rapid Transit Association	TMS	Tramway Museum Society
LRTL	Light Railway Transport League	VAMBAC	Variable automatic multinotch brakes and acceleration control
LTT	Lancastrian Transport Trust		

ACKNOWLEDGEMENTS

This book is based around the photographic collection held by the Online Transport Archive primarily. The photographers concerned or their collections are: the late Geoffrey Ashwell; the late C. Carter; the late Les Collings; the late Gerald Druce; the late Marcus Eavis; Les Folkard; the late Philip Hanson; the late D.W. K. Jones; the late R.W.A. Jones; the late J. Joyce; the late Harry Luff; the late John Meredith; the late Geoffrey Morant; the late Derek Norman; the late Phil Tatt; Alan Murray-Rust; the late Ian Stewart; the late Julian Thompson; Geoffrey Tribe; the late F.E.J. Ward; the late Peter Williams and the late Reg Wilson. The Online Transport Archive now also accommodates the LRTA (London Area) Collection, which includes photographs taken by the late W.J. Wyse and the late Frank Hunt. Other images come the author's collection or from the National Tramway Museum (the late Maurice O'Connor and the late R.B. Parr). As with my other books, I'd like to thank Martin Jenkins for his comments and corrections, and Mike Russell and Ed Spinger for additional illustrations.

Peter Waller
Shrewsbury
October 2020

THE EARLY YEARS

By the start of the 1930s, Blackpool, like so many other tramway systems nationwide, was facing a dilemma. Its existing tramcar fleet was increasingly aged and the contemporary fashion was to regard the tram as out-dated. The Blackpool system had two core components: the Promenade route from Starr Gate to Fleetwood, which handled vast number of holidaymakers during the season; and the 'town' routes to places like Layton and Marton. The latter routes were considered at risk of conversion at the time and it may well have been that, had Walter Luff not been appointed the new general manager in January 1933, the trams featured in this book might not have appeared.

On 27 March 1933, Luff presented his five-year plan for the future of the system – *Special Report Regarding the Transport Undertaking* – to the transport committee. He envisaged the modernisation of the Promenade route – his report commented 'there is no system at present in vogue as capable of dealing with dense crowds as electric cars' – but only basic maintenance for the remainder of the system whilst its future was decided. Earlier – on 21 February 1933 – he had already shown the draft designs of a proposed streamlined car to the committee. The council was persuaded to fund, at the cost of £2,000, the production of a prototype streamlined car and No 200, built by English Electric (whose sales manager, William Lockhart Marshall, had already started to develop the concept of a modern tram for Blackpool prior to Luff's appointment), was formally unveiled on 19 June 1933, contemporaneously with a meeting of the Conference of the Municipal Tramways and Transport Association in the town, having arrived only a matter of hours earlier. When initially recorded for publicity purposes, No 200 was fitted with a pantograph, but this had been replaced by a conventional trolleypole prior to its introduction in Blackpool.

The new tram could accommodate forty-eight seated passengers in two saloons either side of the centre doors; four folding seats were also provided on the central platform but these were soon removed. It was fitted with EE-built 4ft 0in bogies and the same company's Type 305A motors rated at 57hp and Z4 controllers. To emphasise the break with the past, the tram appeared in a new green – rather than red – livery. Having been formally launched, No 200 entered public service on 24 June 1933.

The success of the new car resulted in an order being placed for an additional twenty-four cars – Nos 201-24 – on 26 June 1933; these were to cost £2,356 each and differed only slightly from the prototype car in being 2ft 0in longer in order to improve leg room in the cramped cramped drivers' cabs and to permit an increase in seating capacity. On 13 October 1933, No 200 made its first appearance in St Anne's Square, on the Lytham system, for use of a private hire trip from there to Fleetwood and return; unfortunately, with the desire of Lytham St Anne's to replace its trams with buses – achieved in 1937 – the idea of regular use of the 'Railcoaches' south to Lytham was not to be achieved.

Nos 201 and 202 entered service on 23 December 1933, with No 203 following on 6 January 1934; all 24 were in service by the end of 1934 and had taken over the Lytham Road route from Squires Gate to Gynn Square on 1 March 1934. A minor problem with the frames of the EE-built bogies required slight modification the following year.

With the 'Railcoaches' now in service, Luff sought replacements for two older types of tram; the seasonal 'Toastracks' and the 'Dreadnoughts'. The transport committee sanctioned the construction of two further prototype cars on 25 September 1933. These were built by EE – the single-deck 'Luxury Toastrack' (or 'Boat' as they became known later) No 225 and the double-deck 'Luxury Dreadnought' No 226

THE EARLY YEARS • 9

The prototype of the streamlined trams – No 200 – seen when brand-new in June 1933. D.W.K. Jones Collection/Online Transport Archive

10 • THE BLACKPOOL STREAMLINED TRAMS

A total of 13 open-top 'Super Dreadnoughts' were delivered to the corporation during 1934; the first was initially numbered 226 – as seen here – but was quickly renumbered 237, to be followed by Nos 238-49. The original seating capacity was ninety-four, fifty-four on the upper deck and forty on the lower and required a three-man crew. Geoffrey Morant Collection/Online Transport Archive

The first of the 'Luxury Toastracks' – or 'Boats' as they later become known as – was No 225, which – alongside No 226 – was delivered in February 1934. As No 600 and part of the heritage fleet based at Rigby Road, this tram remains operational more than eighty-five years after its introduction to service. Geoffrey Morant Collection/Online Transport Archive

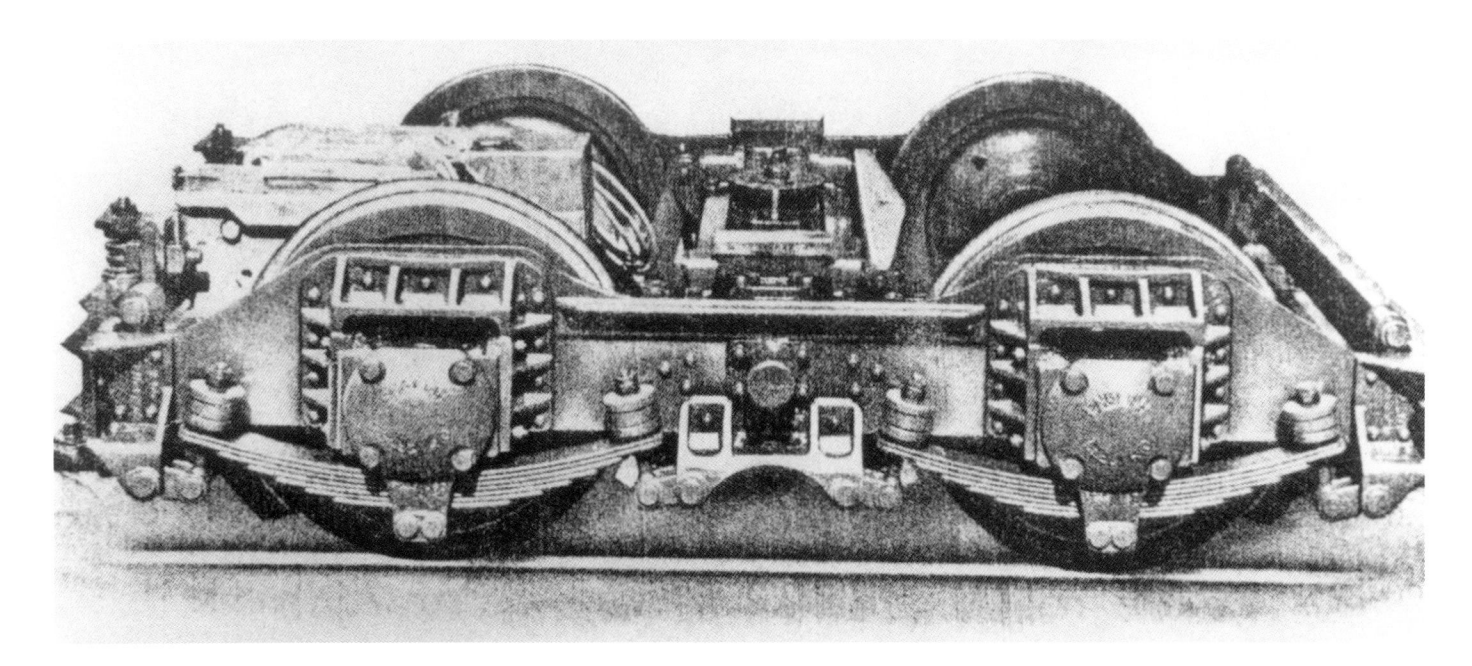

English Electric supplied both the bodies and the bogies for the bulk of the streamlined cars; the latter were either 4ft 0in wheelbase for the single-deck cars or 4ft 9in for the double-deckers. *J. Joyce Collection/Online Transport Archive*

An undated – but relatively early – view of the new 'Railcoaches' in Talbot Square sees two of the type alongside – in the distance – three older double-deck cars. Identifiable in front of the Hotel Metropole are Nos 31 – with the open-balcony top cover – and open-top No 37. The former – one of a batch of fifteen open-top cars supplied by the Midland Railway Carriage & Wagon Co in 1901 – was one of the batch rebuilt as a bogie car and regained its top cover in 1928; it was converted into works car No 4 in 1933 (and was to be preserved on withdrawal). Lytham St Anne's No 37 in its bright blue and cream livery was one of ten open-top trams supplied by the Brush Electrical Engineering Co Ltd in 1905. The presence of the Lytham tram emphasises the fact that the two systems were connected until the final conversion of the Lytham system to bus operation on 28 April 1937. Lytham St. Annes had running powers but no joint services were operated. *D.W.K. Jones Collection/Online Transport Archive*

One of the Series 1 'Railcoaches' is pictured at Bispham alongside single-deck trams from two earlier generations. On the left is 'Crossbench' car No 133; this was one of ten similar cars – Nos 126-135 – that were the amongst the original trams supplied – as Nos 1-10 – to Blackpool & Fleetwood Tramroad Co by G.F. Milnes & Co Ltd in 1898. The section to Fleetwood passed to Blackpool Corporation on 1 January 1920. Two of the 'Crossbench' cars were converted to works use during the Second World War and one of these, No 2, was preserved on final withdrawal and is now part of the NTM collection. The 'Pullman' or 'Pantograph' type were the last new single-deck trams supplied to the corporation before the appointment of Walter Luff. Nos 167-76 were constructed by English Electric as well and were new in 1928. As their name suggests, the cars were originally fitted with pantographs but these were replaced by conventional trolleypoles during 1933. One of the type – No 167 – is also now part of the NTM collection. D.W.K. Jones Collection/Online Transport Archive

(renumbered 237 in August 1934) – appeared in February 1934. Following this, an order for a further eleven single-deck cars and twenty-six double-deckers (twelve open-top and fourteen fully-enclosed) was placed with EE; the total cost was £100,000.

No 226 entered service on 24 February 1934. Although an open-top double-deck car, it was possible to operate as a single-deck car with the upper deck sealed off with special holes in the staircases to permit any water to drain off. The tram was fitted with EE 4ft 9in bogies and two EE Type 327A 40hp motors. Seating capacity was 54 on the upper deck and 40 in the lower. As with No 200, No 237 was slightly shorter than the production cars and also had slightly lower sides.

No 225, which had slightly lower sides than the production batch (and was nicknamed 'Little Willy'), was fitted with EE 4ft 0in bogies and two reconditioned Dick Kerr DK34B 37hp motors. The production batch of 'Boats' – Nos 226 (ii)-236 were delivered during July and August 1934. No 226 (ii) was also fitted with reconditioned Dick Kerr motors whilst the remainder were supplied with two EE 27A 40hp motors. Nos 225 and 226 (ii) were fitted with DB1-K44E controllers whilst Nos 227-36 received reconditioned BTH B18 units. When new, four of the 'Boats' were allocated to Rigby Road for use on the Promenade with the remaining eight based at Marton for use on the circular and coastal tours.

In September 1934, the first of the production batch of 'Luxury Dreadnoughts' was delivered; all had reached Blackpool by the end of October 1934 with the exception of No 249, which remained in Preston for an exhibition and did not enter service until April the following year. Between December 1934 and April 1935, all of the fully-enclosed cars – Nos 250-63 – entered service. Like the earlier 'Luxury Dreadnoughts', these cars were fitted with EE 4ft 9in bogies and 305E motors; the controllers were EE Z6. These cars could seat eighty-four passengers, with forty-four on the upper deck and forty on the lower. The fully-enclosed cars were equipped with opening canvas sun roofs (a feature that was later to disappear). With the installation of check rails, operation of the new double-deck cars on the section from Clifton Drive to Cleveleys was permitted from 8 June 1935. With the fully-enclosed cars being fitted with heaters, the type was employed throughout the year, becoming a regular feature of the Lytham Road route.

The Series 2 'Railcoaches' – Nos 264-83 – were ordered early in 1935 and delivered between June and September the same year. These were outwardly very similar to the earlier cars supplied by EE but were fitted with the EE 305E motors. These arrivals meant that eighty-four new trams had been delivered in two years and had permitted the withdrawal of some older cars and the strengthening of the operational fleet. The withdrawal of the Lytham St Annes trams during 1936 and 1937 resulted in a problem; the operation of that corporation's trams had hidden an increasing capacity problem on the route north from Starr Gate and their withdrawal resulted in the necessity of acquiring additional trams. The withdrawal of the Lytham trams meant that Blackpool now had to handle all traffic on the route between Gynn Square and Starr Gate.

By this date, Marshall had left EE and was working for a number of other companies, including Brush, as a consultant. As a consequence, the order

A busy scene at Gynn Square sees, inter alia, two 'Railcoaches – one heading inbound and one outbound – alongside a Lytham St Anne's double-deck car about to head back towards Lytham and a 'Pantograph' car heading into Dickson Road with a service towards North station. *D.W.K. Jones Collection/Online Transport Archive*

THE EARLY YEARS • 13

for Nos 284-303 went to the Loughborough based manufacturer. Due to copyright issues – EE retained the patents for the original 'Railcoach' design – the new trams differed in detail from their predecessors. The bogies were EMB Hornless 4ft 3in and the motors were Crompton Parkinson C162As rated at 57hp. Controllers were Crompton-West CTJs and, unlike the EE-built cars (which had manually controlled doors), the Brush-built examples were air operated. Seating was again forty-eight, with an additional four on folding seats on the platform; the latter were, however, soon removed. The cars were fitted with sunshine roofs – that could be folded back in good weather – power-operated doors, roof-light windows and wind-down side windows. All twenty entered service between 20 July and 9 October 1937. When new, they were allocated to Rigby Road to operate the Lytham Road service.

Finally, a batch of twelve 'Sun Saloons' – Nos 10-21 – was delivered between August and October 1939. Designed to replace Nos 126-38 – the old 'Cross Bench' cars originally supplied by G.F. Milnes & Co to the Blackpool & Fleetwood Tramroad Co in 1898 which had been sold to the corporation on 1 January 1920 – the trams were constructed by English Electric on the same manufacturer's bogies. These cars were fitted with half-height windows, folding roofs, wooden seats for fifty-six passengers and had no driver's partitions. They were equipped with BTH B265C motors reused from older cars and reconditioned English Electric DB1-K53E controllers. Planned to supplement the 'Boats' and other cars for summer services along the sea front, storm clouds elsewhere in Europe rendered the type redundant even as they were entering service.

The onset of war in September 1939 brought the tram operation new challenges. Initially, the war saw a reallocation of trams. The Brush-built cars were transferred from Rigby Road to Bispham

A 'Boat' heads northbound at Central Pier as the crowds enjoy the various entertainments that the pier had to offer as well as the beach and promenade. The pier predated the tramway by almost twenty years, being originally opened on 30 May 1868; its original manager was also coxswain of the lifeboat based in the adjacent RNLI station. Although the pier is still extant, it has undergone considerable changes over the past century. *J. Joyce Collection/Online Transport Archive*

depot – which was reopened as an operational depot in order to disperse the fleet in case of a bomb hitting Rigby Road – for operation of the Fleetwood to North station route, alongside the 'Pantograph' class, and for occasional use on the Bispham to Squires Gate service.

One of the main challenges was that a fleet designed to cater for huge numbers of holidaymakers was ill-suited to provide transport through the whole year, particularly when the number of out-of-season travellers was destined to increase substantially. Between 1939 and 1943 the number of passengers doubled and the problem of an unsuitable fleet was exacerbated by staff shortages, which prevented the operation of many trams, and by the requirement to run special duties. One of these was the movement of troops under training to the ranges at Rossall. The trams allocated to this duty were the twelve 'Sun Saloons' and their flimsy protection against the harsh weather that the Irish Sea could throw up led to many complaints (the trams were nicknamed 'cattle trucks' by the poor unfortunate soldiers who were forced to use them); as a result, all were rebuilt during 1942 with fixed roofs, full-height windows and driver's partitions. Subsequently more comfortable seating was also fitted. One consequence of this work was a reduction in seating capacity to forty-eight. They did, however, retain their wooden seats until their conversion into VAMBAC cars after the war.

The 'Sun Saloons' were not alone in being rebuilt during the war; the open-top 'Luxury Dreadnoughts' were also to receive treatment. Between August 1941, when No 249 was treated, and June 1942, when No 237 was completed, all thirteen were rebuilt as fully enclosed; this work made them look virtually indistinguishable from the fully-enclosed 'Balloon' class – except that they lacked the canvas roofs – but had the consequence of reducing seating capacity on the upper deck from fifty-four to forty-four.

A view looking north at Talbot Square in the late 1930s sees no fewer than five of the then new streamlined trams in service. Closest to the camera are two of the fully-enclosed double-deck cars; the southbound car partially obscures an open-top 'Luxury Dreadnought' heading north. In the distance can be seen two 'Railcoaches'. The weather seems set fair as the nearest three fully-enclosed trams all have their roofs open to the elements, allowing passengers to get the full benefit of the sun and sea air. *J. Joyce Collection/Online Transport Archive*

16 • THE BLACKPOOL STREAMLINED TRAMS

One of the 'Luxury Dreadnoughts' – No 242 – is pictured in its pre-war condition. Like all of the open-top streamlined double-deck cars No 242 was to be fully enclosed during the Second World War. Renumbered 705 in 1968, this tram was destined to be withdrawn following a collision with No 706 in July 1960 and subsequently scrapped. Its trucks were used in the restoration of Liverpool No 762 and other parts used to restore No 706 to service. *D.W.K. Jones Collection/Online Transport Archive*

Recorded at North Pier in 1940 is one of the 'Luxury Dreadnoughts'; between August 1941 and June 1942 all of these open-top trams were converted to fully enclosed.
Maurice O'Connor/NTM

THE POST-WAR YEARS

By the end of the war, the Blackpool fleet comprised almost forty traditional 'Standard' double-deck cars that dated originally to the 1920s, six single-deck toastrack cars of 1927, ten 'Pullman' cars of 1928 and the 116 modern cars supplied during the 1930s. Following the wartime modifications, the latter comprised sixty-five 'Railcoaches', twelve 'Boats', twenty-seven 'Balloons' and the twelve rebuilt 'Sun Saloons'. Whilst elsewhere the tram was in retreat, in Blackpool, with a relatively modern fleet, there was no major pressure for conversion to bus or trolleybus operation. Two routes – that to Layton and along Central Drive – had been converted during the 1930s but the arrival of the modern cars and Luff's influence had seen the remainder of the town routes survive. There was, however, a potential threat to the Marton route, where the existing track required replacement.

During 1946 and 1947, Series 1 'Railcoach' No 208 underwent a number of experiments which saw it eventually emerge with VAMBAC equipment, which was to be situated at the base of the trolley tower. Seen here on 26 October 1947 prior to the installation of the VAMBAC but after being fitted with M&T HS44 bogies, the car had previously been used – on 14 September 1947 – on an LRTL tour; although the weather was inclement, the 60 or so participants on the trip were impressed by the ride on the new bogies. Norman Forbes, who reported on the tour for *Modern Tramway* noted that 'the magnificently smooth and silent running of No. 208 made a great impression on everyone'. R.B. Parr/NTM

18 • THE BLACKPOOL STREAMLINED TRAMS

The interior of one of the 'Sun Saloons' pictured in the spring of 1949. Phil Tatt/Online Transport Archive

THE POST-WAR YEARS • 19

Brush-built No 292 stands at Claremont Park, on the northern section of the Promenade, with a service towards Thornton Gate. Note the sign promoting that year's illuminations incorporated into the tram's trolleybase. No 292 would become No 629 under the 1968 renumbering scheme. *John Meredith/Online Transport Archive*

'Balloon' No 259 heads southbound at Gynn Square on 16 April 1949. One of the fourteen cars fully-enclosed from delivery. No 259 was new in February 1935. It was destined to become No 722 under the 1968 renumbering scheme. *John Meredith/Online Transport Archive*

As work is undertaken on the track, a 'Railcoach' approaches Gynn Sqaure as it heads north along Dickson Road on 16 April 1949.
John Meredith/Online Transport Archive

THE POST-WAR YEARS • 21

'Boat' No 235 heads north at Claremont Park, on the Promenade, with a service towards Cabin on 16 April 1949. New in August 1934, No 235 was to become No 606 in the 1968 renumbering scheme. *John Meredith/Online Transport Archive*

Work is in hand on one of the 'Balloon' cars in the paint shop at Rigby Road on 16 April 1949. *John Meredith/Online Transport Archive*

Pictured heading along Whitegate Drive in front of Marton depot is converted 'Sun Saloon' No 12. John Meredith/Online Transport Archive

It's obviously a warm day judging by the wide open windows on this converted 'Sun Saloon' pictured outside Marton depot during the spring of 1949. The depot was used to store trams out of season. Phil Tatt/Online Transport Archive

On 17 April 1949, the LRTL operated a tour of the Blackpool system using two of the Series 1 'Railcoaches' – Nos 208, which had by this date been converted to operate using the VAMBAC system, and No 217 – and pair are seen here at Fleetwood. John Meredith/Online Transport Archive

Recorded at Talbot Square on 11 May 1949 are No 11 and 'Standard' No 152. Although the two trams were only built just over a decade apart – No 11 in August 1939 and the 'Standard' in 1925 – the contrast in styles is very apparent. Production of the 'Standards' continued through until 1929 with the completion of No 177; the first impressions of the new streamlined cars less than four years later must have been dramatic. Julian Thompson/Online Transport Archive

24 • THE BLACKPOOL STREAMLINED TRAMS

Pictured on 19 May 1950 at Bispham, these views of 'Balloon' No 262 and Series 1 'Railcoach' show to good effect the predominantly green livery worn by the streamlined cars prior to the appointment of Joseph Franklin as general manager in June 1954. *C. Carter/Online Transport Archive (Both)*

THE POST-WAR YEARS • 25

Luff remained positive about the future of the network and commented during the summer of 1945 that the trams had performed well during the war. He could see few advantages in replacing the trams on the Marton route with trolleybuses, as had been proposed, moreover, his views were borne out in 1946 when the cost of tramway renewal on the route was found to be £12,000 less than the cost of a trolleybus replacement service and offered a fifteen-year, rather than ten-year, life. In January 1947, permission to relay the Marton route was given, with work commencing in June 1949.

During 1946 and 1947, two of the 'Railcoaches' – Nos 208 and 303 – were subject to experimentation. In December 1946, No 208 received initially a set of Maley & Taunton HS44 bogies with resilient wheels; these were subsequently replaced by a set of bogies fitted with worm gears and four 45hp Crompton Parkinson CP90A2 motors and, in December, Crompton Parkinson VAMBAC control equipment was installed. This equipment was designed to permit fast and smooth acceleration and braking, particularly in the town centre, and was also much quieter than conventional control equipment. No 303 was also fitted with Maley & Taunton 6ft 0in bogies and four CP90A2 motors. Initially, it was fitted with CT/TJ controllers but these were subsequently replaced by VAMBAC equipment. Both cars received modified HS44 bogies in 1952. No 303 was not a great success amongst the crews; its air-operated doors made it slower in service and, as a result, it spent much of its life as a VAMBAC car, largely unused in Bispham depot where it was treated as a 'tram of last resort'. Tests on No 208 indicated that it could out-accelerate a contemporary bus, achieving 30½mph in seventeen seconds rather than twenty-three for the bus.

Recorded on the same day as Nos 217 and 262 but at Talbot Square as the conductor has just swung the trolleypole round, is 'Sun Saloon' No 10. By this date, No 10 had been upgraded but not yet fitted with the VAMBAC equipment – which would be housed under the trolley tower when so equipped – and is seen alongside 1924-built 'Standard' No 149. *C. Carter/Online Transport Archive*

26 • THE BLACKPOOL STREAMLINED TRAMS

Two generations of Blackpool tram stand at Fleetwood in September 1950; on the left is 'Pantograph' No 168 whilst on the right is the first of the Brush-built 'Railcoaches' No 284. When withdrawn, No 168 was to be used as the basis of the Rocket illuminated tram in 1961. As No 621, the Brush car was to survive in service until the first decade of the twenty-first century – clocking up almost seventy years of service – and is still based in Blackpool as part of the heritage fleet. Geoffrey Ashwell/Online Transport Archive

'Boat' No 232 is seen close to Central station in October 1950. This car was destined to be one of the type withdrawn in 1963 and scrapped five years later. P.N. Williams/Online Transport Archive

THE POST-WAR YEARS • 27

The next cars to receive attention were the rebuilt 'Sun Saloons'; starting in January 1948 with No 10, the twelve cars were progressively fitted with upholstered seats and fluorescent lighting. The last quartet to be treated – commencing with No 20 in June 1950 and concluding with No 17 in March 1951 – the work also included the replacement of the existing bogies with HS44s and the introduction of VAMBAC equipment. Those cars refurbished earlier were also to receive replacement HS44 bogies and VAMBAC equipment; this commenced with No 21 in December 1949 and was completed with No 13 in April 1952.

In order to modify the 'Sun Saloons' – which subsequently became known as 'Marton VAMBACs' – the corporation acquired seventeen sets of equipment from Crompton Parkinson. Allowing for Nos 10-21 plus Nos 208 and 303, three sets were retained as spares. Nos 10-21, along with No 208, were based at Marton depot for operation on the Marton route; they were supplemented in the autumn of 1952 by Nos 212/19/22/69/72/83 which all had had their fixed trolleyheads replaced by swivelling heads; in contrast, No 208 reverted to a fixed head and so was incompatible with operation on the Marton route. Equipment recovered from the converted 'Sun Saloons' was transferred to Nos 168-75. The performance of the VAMBAC system allied to the quality of the recently relaid track on the Marton route resulted in some very spirited operation.

On 20 June 1954, Walter Luff retired, to be replaced by Joseph Franklin. The early 1950s witnessed a change of livery; the predominantly green scheme was replaced by one that was largely cream with green. The first tram to bear Franklin's name as general manager was No 259; this was also the first of the 'Balloon' class to appear in the new livery and, on 14 October 1954, the first of the type to appear on the Marton route. The single-deck cars soon appeared in the new livery; by the summer of 1954 all bar Nos 206/13/74/90 were in the new scheme although it took longer for the 'Balloons' to be completed – by the summer of 1959 five – Nos 242-44/46/48 – were still in the older style livery.

New in December 1934, 'Balloon' No 255 heads south at North Shore in October 1950 with a service towards Squires Gate. This car was to become No 718 in the 1968 renumbering scheme. P.N. Williams/Online Transport Archive

28 • THE BLACKPOOL STREAMLINED TRAMS

'Sun Saloon' No 20 – pictured here at Talbot Square – was amongst the last of the type to be converted to the VAMBAC system; in fact the work had only been completed four months earlier when caught here in October 1950. *P.N. Williams/Online Transport Archive*

A close-up of one of the HS44 trucks recorded after the appointment of Joseph Franklin. *F.E.J. Ward/Online Transport Archive*

'Balloon' No 257 – later No 720 – is seen at Squires Gate in October 1950. Services along Lytham Road to Squires Gate were to continue until 29 October 1961. *P.N. Williams/Online Transport Archive*

The last of the Series 2 'Railcoaches' – No 283 – stands at the shelter on the Starr Gate loop awaiting departure with a service towards Talbot Square in October 1950. Becoming No 620 in 1968, the tram was eventually rebuilt as OMO car No 2 following withdrawal in 1970.
P.N. Williams/Online Transport Archive

30 • THE BLACKPOOL STREAMLINED TRAMS

Brush-built No 297 is seen approaching the shelter at Starr Gate terminus in October 1950. Becoming No 634 in 1968, the tram was preserved following withdrawal. P.N. Williams/Online Transport Archive

Recorded on the terminal road at Central station in August 1951 are, on the left, 'Railcoach' No 205 and, on the right, 'Boat' No 232. The former was destined to be withdrawn in 1962 and scrapped in July the following year; the latter was withdrawn in 1963 and scrapped five years later. Phil Tatt/Online Transport Archive

THE POST-WAR YEARS • 31

A small boy eyes the photographer with suspicion in this view of the interior of one of the 'Sun Saloons' – No 21 – following its conversion to VAMBAC operation. The photograph shows to good effect the modifications completed during the war. The moquette-covered seats replaced the earlier wooden seats as part of the process to convert the cars to VAMBAC operation. Geoffrey Ashwell/Online Transport Archive

'Boat' No 227 pictured outside Marton depot. The depot here dated originally to 1901 but was extended in 1912. It remained an operational depot until the conversion of the Marton route to bus operation on 28 October 1962 but was used thereafter for a period for the scrapping of withdrawn trams. Following final closure, the site was sold and redeveloped as a filling station. No 227 was the third 'Boat' to be delivered – in July 1934 and was to become No 602 as part of the renumbering in 1968; it remains at Rigby Road as part of the heritage fleet. Geoffrey Ashwell/Online Transport Archive

32 • THE BLACKPOOL STREAMLINED TRAMS

Recorded heading north at Little Bispham in June 1952 is one of the 'Balloon' type. *Geoffrey Ashwell/Online Transport Archive*

Pictured in August 1952, but this time at Royal Oak, is 'Sun Saloon' No 14; this was new in August 1939 and, like all of the batch apart from No 10, was withdrawn following the conversion of the Marton route on 28 October 1962. This view shows to good effect the livery, the sunshine roof panels and the VAMBAC equipment installed in the trolleybase. *Phil Tatt/Online Transport Archive*

THE POST-WAR YEARS • 33

Two 'Balloons' – Nos 250 and 251 – are pictured outside Rigby Road depot on 13 June 1954 as a conductor manipulates the bamboo pole used to turn the trolleypoles. R.B. Parr/NTM

THE FRANKLIN ERA

Virtually the final act of the Luff era was the acquisition of the 'Coronation' cars; these twenty-five single-deck trams were built by Charles Roberts & Co Ltd of Horbury, near Wakefield. Fitted with HS44 bogies and VAMBAC control equipment, these trams proved to be both more costly than budgeted and unsuccessful in service. Although problems with these cars were to occupy much time and effort, there was also much undertaken on the earlier streamlined cars.

Unfortunately, this was also the period when the Blackpool system contracted significantly with the conversion of the town routes, resulting in the withdrawal of many of the trams constructed during the 1930s.

Prior to Franklin's appointment, the future of the double-deck cars was by no means secure. Slow to load and looking out of date, the future of the tramway seemed to be based around modern single-deck cars that could operate a more frequent service.

It's a wet April day in 1956 as No 251 stands at North Pier. This was the second of the fully-enclosed streamlined double-deck cars to enter service – in December 1934 – and was destined to become No 714 under the 1968 renumbering. Withdrawn three years later, the tram was used as the basis of the second rebuilt 'Balloon' cars, emerging as No 762 in 1982. *Phil Tatt/Online Transport Archive*

Series 1 'Railcoach' No 216 stands at Squires Gate on 15 June 1956. New in February 1934, No 216 was to achieve more than 30 years in service before withdrawal in 1965 – one of the last of the original batch of streamlined cars to survive. It was one of five of the type to be scrapped in October 1965. *Julian Thompson/Online Transport Archive*

However, Franklin believed that the 'Balloons' could have a future as part of a strategy that saw a number of innovations – such as the reintroduced circular tour and investment in new sponsored illuminated trams – that could make the trams an attraction in their own right. In addition, as a result of improvements to the track north of Bispham – largely the installation of a check rail – the 'Balloons' were permitted to operate through to Fleetwood from 1958.

From the mid-1950s onwards, the 'Balloons' underwent two modifications. Starting in 1955 with No 257, the traditional twin blinds were replaced by a single, centrally placed, blind; this work was eventually completed by 1980 except on Nos 714 and 725 (withdrawn in 1972 and 1971 respectively). Secondly, starting in 1957 on Nos 241 and 247, the bench seats that had been removed during the war from the upper deck were reinstated, restoring a ninety-four seating capacity to the trams. Work was also undertaken on the original fully-enclosed cars, Nos 250-63, on installing extra seats on the upper decks, taking their capacity to ninety-four also. This work was long drawn out and the final cars to be modified were only completed in the early 1990s (No 722 in 1992 followed by No 720).

From the late 1950s, the Brush cars underwent refurbishment. Some appeared with a modified front dome incorporating a single destination blind; as was often the case with subtle changes to the fleet, the conversion to single blinds was long drawn out and it was not until 1980 that the last was completed.

The 'Boats' remained unchanged through the decade until, in 1959, they were fitted with single-piece plastic windscreens in order to offer some protection to the drivers

Whilst trailer operation had been favoured in Britain historically on a number of systems, the practice had not been long-lived. Continental systems, however, were widespread users of trailers and to Franklin they represented another

Four 'Balloon' class cars but three different variations. Closest to the camera is No 245; this had already received the replacement single-piece destination blinds and was carrying the predominantly cream livery introduced earlier in the decade. Alongside is a second car in the new livery, although this one still retains the original twin destination blinds as do the two on the right; these, however, are still sporting the older – predominantly green – livery. *W.J. Wyse/LRTA (London Area) Collection/Online Transport Archive*

relatively low-cost means of increasing capacity. Prior to any development, Franklin travelled to Germany to see trailer operation in practice. In late 1957, work commenced on the conversion of two of the 'Railcoaches' – Nos 275 and 276 – into the prototype twin-car set. Although the majority of both bodies were retained, the front ends were rebuilt with flat ends, similar to the style of the 'Coronation' class, in order to facilitate coupling. The original English Electric bogies were retained, whilst No 275 – designed to act as a trailer – lost its electrical equipment. The set was fitted with a Willison automatic coupler and Westinghouse air brakes. Proudly proclaiming itself as the 'Progress Twin Car' the new twin-car set was launched on 18 January 1958; it entered public service on 9 April 1958 and first appeared on the Promenade route on 24 May 1958.

The success of the operation led the Transport Committee to authorise the purchase of ten purpose-built trailers on 13 March 1959. The contract for the bodies went to MCW; each was to cost £4,883 with the bogies supplied by Maley & Taunton for an additional £2,797 per pair. On 19 July 1960, the first of the new trailers – No T1 – was formally handed over when it and No 277 took an official party on a tour of the system. Each trailer was 43ft 0in in length and could accommodate 66 seated passengers. All of the trailers were completed in the new predominantly cream livery with a green band and all had been delivered by the start of 1961. No T2 entered service on 13 August 1960 and No T3 on 10 September. The last to be received – No T10 – arrived in Blackpool on 23 January 1961.

In order to provide power for the new trailers – Nos T1-T10 – a further eight of the

THE FRANKLIN ERA • 37

'Railcoaches' – Nos 272-74/77-81 – were modified in a style similar to that adopted for No 276; this conversion work was completed in May 1962. On 3 November 1960, No 275 entered Rigby Road Works to have its electrical equipment restored so that it could become the tenth power car.

The theory of the trailer operation was that at quiet times the trailer could be dropped off, leaving only the power car in service, and that operation should be concentrated on the central – busiest – section of the Promenade route. Operationally, however, there was a gap between theory and practice. The lack of a driving cab on the trailer cars meant that they required turning loops to change direction; these were only situated at Pleasure Beach and Starr Gate south of the town and at Little BIspham and Fleetwood to the north. This resulted in potentially a considerable amount of 'dead' mileage. In addition, the system lacked siding space where trailers could be stored during off-peak periods – plus they would have needed modifying (e.g. the fitting of track brakes) – so that further dead mileage was incurred in off-peak periods when the twin-sets returned to Rigby Road in order to drop off the trailers.

Eventually, given that it became increasingly the case that one power car operated with the same trailer, it was decided to create fixed sets, transferring one of the driver's cabs to the trailer car. The first sets to be so treated were Nos 281 and T1 and 274 and T4 in 1965. These were followed by Nos 275 and T5 in early 1966, Nos 676 and 686 (ex-Nos 276 and T6) in mid 1969 and Nos 677 and 687 (ex-Nos 277 and T7) in late 1969. The remaining three sets remained unmodified and the three trailers – by now renumbered 688-90 – were all withdrawn in 1972. The three power cars – Nos 678-80 – continued in operation.

The experience of travelling on a 'Boat' during the summer of 1959 as the conductor collects the fares. With the Tower in the distance, the passengers enjoy the sun as the car heads northwards. Les Folkard/Online Transport Archive

38 • THE BLACKPOOL STREAMLINED TRAMS

On 17 August 1959, a 'Balloon' heads north towards the Tower at Central Pier. Note the unusual livery; a total of six cars – Nos 237/38/42-44/46 – received cream paint on the panelling between the decks. This was primarily to facilitate the introduction of advertising on the side of the vehicles. The pier itself was opened on 30 May 1868 and originally extended some 503 yards into the Irish Sea. Prominent behind the tram is the original theatre built at the landward end of the pier; this was gutted by fire in 1964 and again in 1973. The theatre that exists today was largely the result of modernisation work completed in 1986. Four years later, the pier was further altered by the erection of a Ferris wheel. *Les Folkard/Online Transport Archive*

With the Carlton Hotel in the background, a 'Railcoach' makes its way from Gynn Square along Dickson Road with a service towards Blackpool North station. *LRTA (London Area) Collection/Online Transport Archive*

THE FRANKLIN ERA • 39

Having just passed Blackpool South station – later the terminus of the railway line once the route through to Blackpool Central was closed on 2 November 1964 – on Waterloo Road, one of the single-deck cars approaches the junction with Lytham Road at Royal Oak with a service from Marton heading back towards the town centre. The Lytham Road section south from Royal Oak to Squires Gate closed on 29 October 1961 – the first of the post-war tram to bus conversions. Harry Luff/Online Transport Archive

The experimental twin-car set – No 276 at the front and No 275 modified as a trailer bringing up the rear – seen shortly after conversion in 1958 operating the Coastal Tour. J. Joyce/Online Transport Archive

40 • THE BLACKPOOL STREAMLINED TRAMS

A close-up illustrating the connections and protective links between Nos 275 and 276 when the prototype set was first introduced.
LRTA (London Area) Collection/Online Transport Archive

THE FRANKLIN ERA • 41

The interior of No 275 following its temporary conversion into a trailer car viewed towards No 276; although its electrical equipment was disconnected, internally the car was not modified, retaining its driving cabs at both ends, which facilitated its restoration to powered operation once delivery of the trailers commenced. LRTA (London Area) Collection/Online Transport Archive

Standing at the Fleetwood terminus in about 1960 awaiting departure with a service to North Station via Dickson Road is No 285. Note the route number '1' on a sheet in the nearside cab window. Harry Luff/Online Transport Archive

With a 'Railcoach' on the main Promenade in the background, one of the Marton 'VAMBAC' cars stands at the South Pier terminus of the Marton route in about 1960. This section of route was seasonal with the majority of cars terminating at Royal Oak. The section beyond Royal Oak was last used at the end of the 1961 season. *Harry Luff/Online Transport Archive*

Recorded at the Lytham Road terminus in about 1960 is Series 1 'Railcoach' No 224. One of the handful of this batch to survive to be renumbered – as No 610 – in 1968, No 224 was used as a works car between October 1964 and May 1965. Withdrawn in 1969, the car was eventually converted into OMO car No 3. *Harry Luff/Online Transport Archive*

THE FRANKLIN ERA • 43

As 'Coronation' No 323 stands at the shelters at North Pier prior to heading north towards Thornton Gate, a 'Railcoach' prepares to set off southbound on a short working to Central station on 4 June 1960. Charles Firminger/Bob Bridger Collection/Online Transport Archive

On the same day, another 'Railcoach' approaches North Pier from the south with a service for Bispham. Charles Firminger/Bob Bridger Collection/Online Transport Archive

44 • THE BLACKPOOL STREAMLINED TRAMS

A view south from North Pier on 4 June 1960 sees a 'Railcoach' on the Lytham Road route following a 'Coronation' as a second 'Railcoach' approaches in the distance. *Charles Firminger/Bob Bridger Collection/Online Transport Archive*

One of the services for which the 'Boats' were designed was the circular tour. This service was, however, suspended in 1939 and was not to be reintroduced until 1957. The work to restore the circular tour required the uncovering of the track in Squires Gate Lane, which had been covered over two years earlier. Seen approaching Talbot Square on the reintroduced circular service is one of the 'Boats'; although ridership was encouraging, the final conversion of the Lytham Road route to bus operation on 29 October 1961 meant that the circular tour ceased as well. *LRTA (London Area) Collection/Online Transport Archive*

THE FRANKLIN ERA • 45

The conductor turns the trolley at the North Station terminus prior to the 'Railcoach' heading northwards along Dickson Road. This view was taken before the installation of the trolley reverser at this point in early 1961. LRTA (London Area) Collection/Online Transport Archive

THE YEARS OF RETRENCHMENT

Although the introduction of the trailer cars boded well for the Promenade route, there was less positive new for the surviving town routes. In early 1960, the Highways Committee proposed the withdrawal of trams from North Station/Dickson Road section; this was rejected on the grounds that the track still had over a decade of useful life and the cost of the replacement buses would be far in excess of the value of scrap recovered.

Whilst the initial threat to the Dickson Road route was averted, the state of the track on Lytham Road – last relaid some twenty-five years earlier – was deteriorating. Here it was recognised that the costs involved of relaying - £140,000 – were more than the cost of replacement buses. Thus, on 7 October 1960, the Transport Committee consented to conversion; this was undertaken on 29 October 1961. The final car from Cabin to Squires Gate was No 268 whilst the last from South Pier was No 222 at 11.19pm. The final departure from Squires Gate to Rigby Road at 11.45pm was No 268.

The second of the Brush-built cars – No 285 – stands at the Fleetwood Ferry terminus in October 1961. New in July 1937, this car was to become No 622 in 1968. W.J. Wyse/LRTA (London Area) Collection/Online Transport Archive

THE YEARS OF RETRENCHMENT • 47

In October 1961 two trams stand at the Talbot Square terminus of the route to Marton. Although the trams look outwardly similar, the slight variations in details – particularly the size and location of the windows – allow for that on the left to be identified as a 'Railcoach' and that on the right as a Marton 'VAMBAC'. LRTA (London Area) Collection/Online Transport Archive

Series 2 'Railcoach' No 279 seen here in original condition was destined to be one of ten of the batch to be rebuilt for use as the power cars in the twin-car sets. Renumbered 679 in 1968, the tram was one of the trio that were not modified into a fixed set. Withdrawn in 2004 and initially preserved by the LTT in 2006, the intention was that the car be restored to its original condition. The tram was returned to Blackpool Transport ownership with work still to be completed. W.J. Wyse/LRTA (London Area) Collection/Online Transport Archive

48 • THE BLACKPOOL STREAMLINED TRAMS

By the early 1960s, work was in hand in the modification of the 'Balloon' class from double to single destination. Pictured at Fleetwood on 7 September 1962 are two cars demonstrating the differing styles. Still retaining its original two-blind layout is No 261 (below) whilst No 257 (above) has received the new single-blind display. Nos 257 and 261 were destined to be renumbered 720 and 724 in 1968 whilst, for No 261, a more radical rebuild was to follow in 2004 when it was modified as the fourth – and last – of the 'Millennium' cars. *Les Collings/Online Transport Archive (both)*

The next route to succumb was that to Marton. This was converted to bus operation on 28 October 1962. With the loss of the Marton route, the first significant withdrawals of the streamlined cars commenced. Prior to the conversion, three of the VAMBAC cars had already been withdrawn: No 10 in 1960 as a result of an accident whilst No 14 was withdrawn in 1961 and used as a driver training car and No 21 also succumbed in 1961 for cannibalisation for spare parts. Five of the batch – Nos 11, 13, 15, 17 and 18 – were in operation on the last day of the route. Although No 11 was secured for preservation – and departed for the ill-fated Hayling Island preservation scheme on 9 September 1965 (its requested use on an enthusiast tour in early 1963 meant that it was not sold for scrap alongside the rest of the batch) – the other surviving VAMBAC cars – Nos 12-20 – were amongst seventeen trams sold for scrap. Other casualties at this stage were the two 'Railcoaches' that had had VAMBAC equipment at some stage – Nos 208 and 303 – plus Nos 200/07/10/14/23. All seventeen cars were scrapped in Marton depot; Nos 18, 210 and 223 were amongst the first to be scrapped during February 1963 with the remainder being despatched the following month. Following the closure of Marton depot, the eight 'Boats' allocated there were transferred to Bispham.

The final conversion was to be from North station along Dickson Road; this was converted to bus operation on 27 October 1963. The last car to depart from North Station to Fleetwood at 10.53pm was Brush-built No 290 whilst the official last tram was No 256. Following the conversion of this route, the surviving Brush-built cars were transferred from Bispham depot to Rigby Road for operation from Fleetwood to Starr Gate. The 'Boats' transferred to Bispham the previous year were also reallocated to Blundell Street but the

Recorded in front of Marton depot towards the end of its life is Series 1 'Railcoach' No 219. This had originally been new in February 1934 and was to be one of the type taken out of service following the conversion of the Marton route in October 1962. The tram was scrapped in July 1963. *Marcus Eavis/Online Transport Archive*

50 • THE BLACKPOOL STREAMLINED TRAMS

The first of the double-decks cars – No 237 – is seen standing in front of the Clifton Hotel in Talbot Square in about 1961 prior to heading back to the depot. The hotel, which was Grade II listed in 1974, was originally constructed in 1865 but enlarged in 1874 on the site of the older Clifton Arms Hotel. *Marcus Eavis/Online Transport Archive*

During the summer of 1961 Frankie Vaughan was performing at the Palace Theatre in Blackpool and so this view of Nos 275 and T5 was taken when the trailer was almost brand-new; it had been delivered the previous year. When first introduced, the two-car sets were designed to provide a faster – but limited stop – service and No 275 displays the stops served on the front dash; this feature was, however, relatively short-lived. *Marcus Eavis/Online Transport Archive*

One of the 'Railcoaches' is pictured in front of Bispham depot in about 1962. The depot was originally opened by the Blackpool & Fleetwood Tramway Co on 14 July 1898 and was extended at the rear in both 1902 and 1914. Taken over by the corporation on 1 January 1920, the depot closed on 27 October 1963. Used as a store until January 1966, the structure was finally demolished in 1983. *Marcus Eavis/Online Transport Archive*

end of the season witnessed the withdrawal of four of the 'Boats'; Nos 229/32/32/34 were sent for storage to Blundell Street depot where they were scrapped in April 1968.

With the conversions of the early 1960s and, despite the elimination of all of the pre-streamline era trams, Blackpool still had a surplus in terms of operational trams and, as a result, further withdrawals and disposals followed. All of the first batch of 'Railcoaches' were withdrawn by the end of 1965 with the exception of No 224 – used as a PW car between October 1964 and May 1965 – which was the only one of the batch to receive a post-1969 fleet number – No 610 – and was eventually to be rebuilt emerging as OMO car No 3 in October 1972. A total of 20 were scrapped between December 1961 and October 1965; the exceptions – apart from No 224 – were No 209, which was used to provide the basis of the Santa Fe locomotive (later No 733) in 1962, No 220, which was stored until 1972 and then used as the basis of OMO No 4, No 221, which was converted into a PW car (No 5) in April 1965 and subsequently modified to become OMO No 5 (and subsequently preserved) and No 222, which formed the basis of the Hovertram (later No 735) in 1963.

One of the Brush-built cars stands at the Fleetwood Ferry terminus in about 1962; behind is one of the Roberts-built 'Coronation' cars of 1953, No 309. *Marcus Eavis/Online Transport Archive*

Early 1964 was to witness a further change of livery, with Nos 269/85/88/90/91/96/99, 300 and 301 all appearing with cream below the waist band and green above. By the end of the year, all of the Brush-built cars had been so treated as had two of the Series 2 'Railcoaches' – Nos 269 and 270.

The winter of 1964 saw the nineteen surviving Brush cars in Rigby Road for attention, alongside receiving replacement Z4 controllers, windows and heaters from withdrawn 'Railcoaches' as well as having their sun roofs replaced by fixed panelling. Unfortunately, for No 301 these modifications were not to last long as the car was withdrawn following an accident in 1966 (and scrapped two years later).

The winter of 1965/66 – starting on 29 November – saw the experimental use of three double-deck cars – Nos 240, 257 and 263 – on the winter timetable to see if there was sufficient demand for their use; there was not and the experiment was ended.

More positive news after the round of withdrawals earlier in the decade was the re-emergence of Series 2 'Railcoach' No 264 on 13 January 1966. This tram had been seriously damaged in an accident and was rebuilt using two of the fibre-glass ends that had been originally destined for use in unbuilt eleventh and twelfth trailer car sets with windscreens salvaged from the now withdrawn 'Coronation' No 313 – the first of the unsuccessful type to succumb. Other work to No 264 included the use of replacement ICI Darvic plastic panelling in the body – an attempt to reduce corrosion – and an interior refurbishment. The rebuilt tram was slightly longer than its original 42ft 3in length and

THE YEARS OF RETRENCHMENT • 53

Pictured heading eastbound along Whitegate Drive, at its junction with Lindsay Avenue, is one of the Marton 'VAMBAC' cars making its way towards the South Pier terminus via Waterloo Road and Royal Oak. This service was to be converted to bus operation in October 1962. *Marcus Eavis/Online Transport Archive*

emerged in the new cream and green livery. It also saw an increase in seating capacity from forty-eight to fifty-six.

The second half of the decade witnessed Blackpool trying to resolve the problems with the 'Coronation' cars. A number – Nos 306/10/18-28 – had their VAMBAC equipment replaced by conventional Z4 or Z6 controllers salvaged from withdrawn 'Railcoaches'. Despite these modifications, other issues meant that the surviving VAMBAC cars were all withdrawn by October 1970 and the converted ones by the end of 1975.

At the end of 1968, Blackpool undertook its first ever fleet renumbering; the surviving single-deck cars received numbers in the 600-690 series whilst the twenty-seven double-deck cars became Nos 700-26. The single-deck streamlined trams were Nos 600-07 ('Boats'), 610 (the surviving Series 1 'Railcoach'), 611-18 (the surviving Series 2 'Railcoaches)', Nos 619-38 (the surviving Brush-built 'Railcoaches'; the one exception – No 301 – had been withdrawn in 1966 and scrapped in April 1968), 671-80 (the twin-set power cars) and 681-90 (the twin-set trailers).

In January 1969, a second Series 2 'Railcoach' – No 618 – emerged with modified front ends; in this case, in a forerun of the design adopted for the OMO cars the next decade, its new front ends were tapered. The work on the car saw its seating capacity increased from 48 to 56. Both Nos 611 and 618 were, however, to continue as two-man operated trams; the need to reduce costs of operating the system in the winter period needed a more radical solution.

A second car was also modified during 1969; this was Brush-built No 638. As part of testing for OMO operation, it was fitted with forward entrances, with a consequent reduction in seating capacity to forty-four (plus twenty standing passengers). In its revised form and in an all-cream livery, it re-entered service during 1970. It was completed in the early part of the year but it took some six months before union agreement was reached to permit to operate with only a single-man crew.

The conversion of No 638 was, however, not a success. The design of the entrance door placed it too far back to permit the driver to collect the fares efficiently and the vastly reduced capacity was also a disadvantage; No 638 reverted to two-man operation in 1974.

Following a collision between Brush-built No 628 and 'Balloon' No 726 on 28 September 1969 in which eleven were injured, the former was withdrawn and, during 1970, its underframes were used in the construction of a new works car (No 751). Another accident later in the year saw Nos 703 and 713 collide but both were repaired and returned to service.

In October 1962, one of the Marton 'VAMBAC' cars is pictured in front of Marton depot; the Marton service was converted to bus operation on the 28th of the month. This conversion resulted in the withdrawal and scrapping of all of the surviving 'VAMBAC' cars with the exception of No 11, which was eventually to be preserved. Derek Norman/Online Transport Archive

THE YEARS OF RETRENCHMENT • 55

During August 1963 one of the single-deck cars receives the attention of the tram washer at Rigby Road. Derek Norman/Online Transport Archive

A 'Railcoach' heads northbound along Dickson Road with a service to Fleetwood in October 1963. The North Station to Gynn Square section was the last of the 'town' routes to survive in Blackpool. Derek Norman/Online Transport Archive

56 • THE BLACKPOOL STREAMLINED TRAMS

In October 1963 – shortly before the conversion of the route – No 700 stands on the terminal stub at Blackpool North prior to using the trolley reverser – this had been installed in early 1961 when the North station route was slightly cut back and was first used on 10 March 1961 – and heading towards Gynn Square via Dickson Road. When the 'Balloons' were rebuilt the upper and lower-deck glass louvres were dispensed with. *W.J. Wyse/LRTA (London Area) Collection/Online Transport Archive*

On 27 October 1963 a 'Railcoach' stands at Fleet Ferry awaiting departure with a service to Talbot Square. Alongside is 'Standard' No 160; this was one of the quartet of 'Standards' that were to survive in service until the end of October 1966. *Geoffrey Tribe/Online Transport Archive*

THE YEARS OF RETRENCHMENT • 57

It's 26 October 1963 and time is running out for operation of the Dickson Road section to North station as 'Boat' No 225 is seen on Dickson Road during an enthusiasts' tour. *Geoffrey Tribe/Online Transport Archive*

A contrast in front ends on the Promenade on 27 October 1963 sees No 247 with the new single blind heading northbound whilst twin-blind heads in the opposite direction. No 247 had received its revamped blinds in 1957. In the background the familiar Lewis's department store is under construction; built on the site of the Alhambra Theatre, the store opened in 1964. *Geoffrey Tribe/Online Transport Archive*

58 • THE BLACKPOOL STREAMLINED TRAMS

One of the 'Progress Twin-Car' sets – Nos 274 and T4 – is seen heading northwards on the Promenade to Little Bispham on 26 October 1963. Geoffrey Tribe/Online Transport Archive

THE YEARS OF RETRENCHMENT • 59

Followed by a 'Coronation', one of the 'Railcoaches' heads south in front of the Lewis's store on 26 October 1963 with a service towards the Pleasure Beach. *Geoffrey Tribe/Online Transport Archive*

Pictured heading southbound at North Pier is 'Balloon' No 248 with the modified single-blind front destination. Following the 1968 renumbering scheme, No 247 was to become No 710, surviving until withdrawal in 2008. *Geoffrey Tribe/Online Transport Archive*

60 • THE BLACKPOOL STREAMLINED TRAMS

On 27 October 1963 No 245 heads south on the Promenade towards Pleasure Beach. New in September 1934, No 245 was to become No 708 as part of the 1968 renumbering. *Alan Murray-Rust/Online Transport Archive*

An unidentified 'Railcoach' is seen on Dickson Road at its junction with Mount Street with a service towards North station. This was the final day of tramway service for this section as the route was converted to bus operation. The final closure of the 'town' tramways between 1961 and 1963 was to result in the withdrawal of a number of streamlined cars. Alan Murray-Rust/Online Transport Archive

The last day of the Dickson Road route also saw the end of the summer season in Blackpool and the final running of the cars operated in connection with the illuminations. Here, the 'Santa Fe' train – of which the locomotive was constructed using the frames of Series 1 'Railcoach' No 209 in 1962 – is seen on the Promenade on that fateful evening. Alan Murray-Rust/Online Transport Archive

62 • THE BLACKPOOL STREAMLINED TRAMS

In April 1965, one of the batch of original English Electric-built 'Railcoaches', No 221, which had been withdrawn and stored in 1963, was to emerge as works car No 5. It was to remain on works duties until October 1971 when it was withdrawn again, this time for rebuilding into one of the 13 OMO trams. Retaining its No 5 as an OMO car, the rebuilt tram re-entered service in November 1972. It was to remain in service in this rebuilt guise until withdrawal in 1993; subsequently the tram was preserved and now forms part of the NTM collection, albeit in store and in an unrestored condition. It is pictured here in Rigby Road on 22 May 1966 shortly after its renumbering for works duties. R.L. Wilson/Online Transport Archive

The upper-deck interior of a 'Balloon' – believed to be No 254 – in September 1965. Les Folkard/Online Transport Archive

THE YEARS OF RETRENCHMENT • 63

It is the early autumn of 1965 and No 299 is recorded awaiting departure with a service to Bispham. New in September 1937, No 299 was to be become No 636 under the 1968 renumbering scheme. Harry Luff/Online Transport Archive

Standing at Bispham awaiting its next duty on 28 June 1967 is 'Boat' No 233. Destined to become No 605 in the following year's renumbering scheme, the 'Boat' was initially preserved by the LTT, spending some time based at Beamish, before it was sold to San Francisco in 2013. It has subsequently been restored to its original 1930s livery and renumbered back to 233. Geoffrey Tribe/Online Transport Archive

64 • THE BLACKPOOL STREAMLINED TRAMS

Passengers board 'Balloon' No 259 at Pleasure Beach on 28 June 1967; behind the double-decker is one of the 'Coronation' class. No 259 was to become No 722 the following year. One of the relatively few of the type not to survive in some form, No 722 was scrapped in 2009. *Geoffrey Tribe/Online Transport Archive*

No 264 was the first of the Series 2 'Railcoaches' in June 1935 and is seen here at Pleasure Beach on 28 June 1967; it had been rebuilt during 1966 using plastic panelling and incorporating the modified front ends as used on the twin-sets. The rebuilt car, at 42ft 8in in length, was six inches longer than when new. The use of the plastic panels was an attempt to solve the problem caused by Blackpool's climate to the traditional paint finish. The car was to become No 611 under the 1968 renumbering scheme. *Geoffrey Tribe/Online Transport Archive*

THE YEARS OF RETRENCHMENT • 65

On 26 August 1967 the last of the Series 1 'Railcoaches' – No 224 approaches the Fleetwood Ferry terminus. Used as a works car for a period between October 1964 and May 1965, this was the only one of the original batch of EE-built trams to carry its allocated new a fleet number – No 610 – under the 1968 renumbering scheme. *Alan Murray-Rust/Online Transport Archive*

Also on 26 August 1967, No 245 is recorded in front of Rigby Road depot; this tram was to become No 708 under the 1968 renumbering scheme. *Alan Murray-Rust/Online Transport Archive*

66 • THE BLACKPOOL STREAMLINED TRAMS

Seen approaching the Starr Gate terminus on 26 August 1967 is No 297; becoming No 634 in 1968, this was one of five of the type withdrawn at the end of the 2004 season that were not to be later restored to service. It does, however, survive in preservation locally. *Alan Murray-Rust/Online Transport Archive*

Heading southbound towards Talbot Square is Series 2 'Railcoach' No 266 on 26 August 1967. Renumbered 613 in 1968, the tram was withdrawn in 1973 and was subsequently rebuilt as OMO No 9. Re-entering service in December 174, the car was finally withdrawn in 1987 and scrapped in July the following year. *Alan Murray-Rust/Online Transport Archive*

THE YEARS OF RETRENCHMENT • 67

Seen at Victoria Square, Cleveleys, on 26 October 1968 is newly-renumbered No 620, the last of the Series 2 'Railcoaches' to be built by EE. Prior to the renumbering scheme, this car had been No 283. Withdrawn in 1972, the tram was subsequently rebuilt as OMO No 2. John Meredith/Online Transport

In January 1969 one of the Series 2 'Railcoaches' – No 618 – emerged with modified front ends; as such the car presaged the design adopted late by the 13 OMO cars. The newly-rebuilt car is pictured here in August 1969. H. Luff/Online Transport Archive

INTO THE 1970s

By the end of the 1960s, seven of the twin-car sets were now operating in fixed formations; by the end of 1970 the three power cars – Nos 678-80 – that had not been modified were operating over the winter without their trailers. The three associated trailers – Nos 688-90 – were withdrawn in 1972 but were retained in store for a period thereafter. No 688 was subsequently scrapped but Nos 689 and 690 were sold to GEC for experimental purposes in November 1981 at £800 each. The two were sold three years later for preservation at the West Yorkshire Transport Museum and moved to Bradford. The museum, which morphed into the ill-fated Transperience project at Low Moor, was forced to retrench in the late 1980s and this resulted in the disposal – and scrapping – of the two trailer cars during the summer of 1989.

Having arrived at its destination, Series 2 'Railcoach' No 619 is pictured at Pleasure Beach on 30 May 1970. New originally as No 282 in August 1935, No 619 was rebuilt as OMO car No 7 following withdrawal in 1972. It emerged in its new guise in July 1973. Withdrawn for a second time in 1987, it was subsequently rebuilt as the fake crossbench car No 619, being relaunched in that form in August the same year. Geoffrey Tribe/Online Transport Archive

Seen at Fleetwood on 16 November 1969 is No 630; this was one of only three of the Brush-built cars that were not withdrawn or stored at the end of the 2004 season. Surviving until the end of the traditional tramway in 2011, No 630 was repainted into the standard livery it carried during the 1990s prior to preservation at Crich. *Alan Murray-Rust/Online Transport Archive*

In a foretaste for the future of the system, in early 1971, 'Boat' No 601 was fitted experimentally with pantograph; this was not to last and the tram reverted to normal trolleypole operation later in the year. Withdrawn during 1971, No 601 was to become the first Blackpool tram to cross the Atlantic. It was initially sent across to the USA for a trade fair but its visit was made permanent when it was sold to the Western Railway Museum, Suisin City, California. One of the features of the operation of the 'Coronation' class was the illuminated advertising panels carried above the roof; in another trial, modified 'Railcoach' No 611 was fitted with these panels from a withdrawn 'Coronation' class. Deemed a success, as other 'Coronation' cars were withdrawn so they also surrendered their advertising panels to the surviving 'Railcoaches'.

Although experiments with Nos 611, 618 and 638 had not been wholly successful, the corporation was still determined to proceed with plans to convert certain cars to one-person operation. Investigation indicated that the Brush-built cars were unsuitable for conversion and so the programme concentrated on the surviving older EE-built 'Railcoaches'. The initials cars for the conversion programme were Nos 610, 616, 617 and 620 along with No PW5, which was taken out of service in early 1972 as a result of body defects and replaced as a works car by Brush-built No 624, and unrenumbered 220, which had been in store since withdrawal in 1963.

The revised trams were designed by the corporation's then chief engineer, Alan H. Williams. The work in conversion included the replacement of the original ends with tapered ends similar to those fitted to No 618, which incorporated the entrance doors and the small driver's cab, extending the underframe and the replacement of the traditional-style tram seats with back-to-back bus seats. The resulting trams were longer than originally built – at 48ft – and could accommodate forty-eight seated passengers plus up to sixteen standing; originally it had been planned to accommodate fifty seated but this was altered during conversion to permit easier passenger movement. The length of the OMO cars meant that they were also fitted with slightly longer trolleypoles.

The first of the OMO cars was launched on 7 March 1972; this initially appeared as No 616 but it was soon to be renumbered 1. Whilst work on the conversion of the first six – to be Nos 1-6 – was in hand during 1972, authorisation for the conversion of a further seven cars – Nos 611-15/18/19 – was given and these were destined to become Nos 7-13, with the last being completed in June 1976. With the introduction of the winter service on 30 October 1972, five of the OMO cars – in their striking new plum and custard livery – took over the Starr Gate to Fleetwood service. The OMO cars shared the winter timetable with some of the Brush-built cars until 1975 when there were sufficient OMO cars in service to ensure that they were able to operate all the winter timetable diagrams.

During the programme to construct the OMO cars there were minor modifications; the most significant of these was the adoption – on No 10 in April 1975 – of Metalastik suspension. This was successful and resulted in the increase in tyre life from 60,000 to 100,000 miles; as a result, the equipment was gradually fitted to the other cars in the OMO fleet. No 10 was also the first of the OMO cars to appear in a new red and cream livery; the earlier plum and custard livery had not proved successful in service as it was prone to rapid fading. The first of the original OMO cars to appear in the revised livery was No 4. In 1975 No 678, one of the former twin-set power cars now devoid of a trailer, was fitted experimentally with a Bracknell Willis pantograph following work on the realignment of the overhead between Starr Gate and Thornton Gate to permit pantograph operation; this was followed by the use of pantographs on OMO cars Nos 4, 5 and 13 in 1976. However, as earlier in the decade, the experiment proved unsuccessful and all eventually reverted to trolleypole operation. No 678 regained its trolleypole in May 1976 and the others reverted during 1977 and 1978.

The management of the tramway underwent a further change in the early 1970s; in the summer of 1973, Stuart Pillar was appointed chief engineer whilst the following spring saw Derek Hyde replace Joseph Franklin as general manager. It was to be the former who undertook the design of the two rebuilt double-deck 'Balloon' cars as Nos 761 and 762.

The next Brush-built car to be withdrawn was No 629 in 1972; the tram was to be stored pending a decision on its future until 1980, when it was scrapped. This was followed during 1974 by the withdrawal of another of the Brush-built cars – No 635 (ex-298) – which was offered to, and accepted by, the TMS for preservation although it has led a somewhat peripatetic existence since then and it is still under restoration. It is currently anticipated that a full restoration will be commenced in mid-2020. This car had been fitted with CP C162A motors (in place of the EE EE305s fitted in 1965) and Allen West CT/TJ controllers prior to preservation, thus restoring much of the equipment to that which had been originally installed when the car was new.

In early 1976, a second 'Boat' – No 603 – made its way across the Atlantic; its destination was Philadelphia, where it was to assist in the bicentenary celebrations for the anniversary of the US Declaration of Independence, having been regauged to the SEPTA gauge of 1,581mm. No 603 returned from the USA on 12 July 1977 still in the special livery carried in Philadelphia. During 1977 there were reports that No 607 – which had been taken out of service in 1972 – was to be transferred to a museum in the USA; in the event, No 607 was reprieved and returned to service. Following final withdrawal in 2004, No 607 was to be preserved at Crich.

The summer of 1977 witnessed two accidents. On 26 June, Nos 7 and 637 collided at Derby Baths whilst on 6 July, Nos 705 and 710 met at Barton Avenue. The force of the collision was sufficient to damage the frames of No 705 but all four were returned to service after repair. During the summer of 1977, a number of the Brush-built cars – Nos 622/23/27/31/34/37 – were fitted with replacement EE ZB1Z6 controllers salvaged from withdrawn 'Coronation' class cars.

Two 'Balloons' – Nos 714 and 725 – had been withdrawn in 1971; these were to form the basis of Stuart Pillar's two 'new' double-deck cars, Nos 762 and 761 respectively. No 761 was formally launched on 4 July 1979. The new body was built around the teak framing of the original car, with extensions provided by Metal Sections Ltd. The actual construction was handled in Rigby Road. The original bogies were substantially rebuilt to allow for a 5ft 6in wheelbase and the use of Metalastik suspension. Westinghouse chopper control was adopted although the original EE305 motors were retained. The body was provided with a single forward entrance on both sides. The use of a single door was to cause significant delays. Although originally designed to accommodate one-hundred seated passengers, this was reduced to 98 in order to improve passenger flow. Fitted with a pantograph from new, No 761 entered service on 2 July 1979.

With work completed on No 761, attention shifted to No 762. This car was stripped for the conversion work during the summer of 1980 but work was delayed and the car was not completed until early 1982; tested in April that year, the rebuilt car was formally inspected by the Department of Transport on 27 May 1982. In terms of design, the major difference between the two rebuilt cars was that No 762 retained central exits; this had the result of reducing its capacity to ninety seated passengers (fifty-six on the upper deck and thirty-four on the lower). Nos 761 and 762 became known as the 'Jubliee' cars.

Recorded making use of the loop at Pleasure Beach on 30 May 1970 is No 719. This car, suitably modified, is now one of nine of the type that are allocated to Blackpool Transport's B fleet to operate alongside the new 'Flexity' units. Geoffrey Tribe/Online Transport Archive

72 • THE BLACKPOOL STREAMLINED TRAMS

Also recorded on 30 May 1970, this time standing in Rigby Road depot, is No 638 in all-cream livery. This car had been converted the previous year to form a second experimental OMO tram; fitted with forward entrances, which reduced the seating capacity to forty-four (plus twenty standing), the modified car re-entered service in 1970. The experiment was not a success, however, and the car reverted to normal two-person operation in 1974. No 638 was finally withdrawn in 1980 and scrapped three years later. Geoffrey Tribe/Online Transport Archive

Collecting the fares on the top deck of a 'Balloon' in May 1970.
Geoffrey Tribe/Online Transport Archive

INTO THE 1970s • 73

In the early autumn of 1970, Brush-built No 637 passes in front of the North Euston Hotel at Fleetwood as it approaches the Fleetwood Ferry terminus. The driver has already set the destination blind for the return journey to Starr Gate. Designed by Decimus Burton, the Grade II listed North Euston Hotel was built during 1840 and 1841 as part of a grandiose plan to create the planned town of Fleetwood as a major seaside resort and stopping off point for travellers between England and Scotland in an era when there were no main lines across the border and taking a steamer from Fleetwood northwards was the only option. The completion of the West Coast main line over the next decade rendered the plans obsolete and the hotel was sold to the government, which used it for a number of military purposes. It reverted to being a hotel in 1898 – the same year that the tramway from Blackpool to Fleetwood was opened. Marcus Eavis/Online Transport Archive

74 • THE BLACKPOOL STREAMLINED TRAMS

With Blundell Street depot in the background, one of the unmodified twin-car sets – Nos 678 and 688 – stand on Blundell Street in the early autumn of 1970. Opened by the Blackpool Electric Tramways Co on 12 September 1885 to house the company's pioneering conduit electric trams, the depot passed to the corporation on 10 September 1892. The depot was rebuilt in 1898 and used as workshops until the opening of the new works at Rigby Road in 1920. The construction of the depot at Rigby Road resulted in Blundell Street being increasingly used as a store for withdrawn trams. It was finally demolished in 1982. *Marcus Eavis/Online Transport Archive*

Two of the Brush-built cars – No 629 closest to the camera and No 623 in the distance – are seen at Manchester Square on 6 February 1971. By this date, No 629 was approaching the end of its life; withdrawn the following year, it was scrapped in November 1972. No 623, however, was to survive until the new millennium and, following withdrawal, was preserved at Heaton Park. *John Meredith/Online Transport Archive*

INTO THE 1970s • 75

Brush-built No 623 is pictured at Manchester Square on 6 February 1971. John Meredith/Online Transport Archive

On the same day, sister car No 626 heads south at Pleasant Street, North Shore, with a service towards Manchester Square. John Meredith/Online Transport Archive

76 • THE BLACKPOOL STREAMLINED TRAMS

On 1 June 1971, No 627 stands at Starr Gate; as No 290, this tram had operated the final working from North Station to Fleetwood in October 1963 when the Dickson Road route was converted to bus operation. *Les Folkard/Online Transport Archive*

INTO THE 1970s • 77

Brush-built No 636 approaches the stop at the Starr Gate on 10 July 1971; following withdrawal, this tram was used as a test-bed at Derby. It remains extent in the East Midlands. John Meredith/Online Transport Archive

Recorded at North Pier on 10 July 1971 are the modified OMO No 638 heading south towards Pleasure Beach and twin-car set Nos 675 and 685 heading northbound towards Little Bispham. John Meredith/Online Transport Archive

78 • THE BLACKPOOL STREAMLINED TRAMS

Recorded at North Pier on 10 July 1971 are two of the Brush-built cars – Nos 622 and 630 – along with 'Balloon' No 722. Both of the single-deck cars still survive, although their fates are very different: whilst No 630 is preserved as part of the NTM collection at Crich, No 622 has been converted into a classroom at a local primary school. No 722 does not, however, survive; it was scrapped in 2009.
John Meredith/Online Transport Archive

On a grey day at Fleetwood Ferry – 29 April 1972 – former towing car No 678 picks up passengers prior to heading south back towards Blackpool.
Geoffrey Tribe/Online Transport Archive

INTO THE 1970s • 79

Standing at Fleetwood Ferry on 29 April 1972 is Brush-built No 621; at this date, the tram still retained its original twin destination blinds. *Geoffrey Tribe/Online Transport Archive*

Goodbye No 610 and hello No 3 on 29 April 1972 as work is in progress on the conversion of the Series 1 'Railcoach' into one of the first OMO cars to enter service. The only one of the original streamlined trams to be allocated a number in the 1968 scheme, No 610 had been withdrawn in 1969. Between October 1964 and May 1965 it had been used as a works car. As OMO No 3, it re-entered service in October 1972. *Geoffrey Tribe/Online Transport Archive*

80 • THE BLACKPOOL STREAMLINED TRAMS

Standing in Rigby Road depot on 29 April 1972 is OMO car No 1; at this stage the car had not entered service – it was not to do so until October the same year having been withdrawn from service, prior to rebuilding, as No 616 in 1970. In front can be seen No 619; this was withdrawn during 1972 and subsequently rebuilt as OMO car No 7. *Geoffrey Tribe/Online Transport Archive*

An interior view of the rebuilt front end of OMO car No 1 prior to its entry into service. The extended underframe, required to permit the forward entrance, and to accommodate the fare collection equipment, was the Achilles' Heel of the type as, over a period of time, it resulted in a considerable 'sag' which gave the type a distinctive curvature later in their lives.
Geoffrey Tribe/Online Transport Archive

INTO THE 1970s • 81

Recorded outside Rigby Road depot in April 1972 is Series 2 'Railcoach' No 612. By early 1972, the streamlined cars were starting to be equipped with the illuminated advertising panels that had previously been used on the 'Coronation' class but, by this date, No 612 was approaching the end of its life. Withdrawn later in 1972, the car was subsequently rebuilt as OMO No 8, re-entering service in June 1974. Finally taken out of service, No 8 is the only one of the 13 OMO cars to be preserved in Blackpool. *Frank Hunt/LRTA (London Area) Collection/Online Transport Archive*

82 • THE BLACKPOOL STREAMLINED TRAMS

During 1969, Brush-built No 638 was rebuilt with forward entrances in order to test one-person operation. The car is seen here in this modified condition in its all-cream livery. As a result of discussions with the trade unions, it took some time after the car re-entered service in 1970 before OMO operation commenced. However, No 638 was not a success – the position of the forward doors, for example, was not ideal – and the tram soon reverted to two-man operation. *Frank Hunt/LRTA (London Area) Collection/Online Transport Archive*

Pictured heading southbound during the summer of 1972 is the unique No 618. The tram is passing the Lewis's department store; this had opened in 1964, having been built on the site of the old Alhambra, and was to survive until 1993. Subsequently, the top two floors were removed and the surviving structure reclad in brick. As such it is still extant today. *Philip Hanson/Online Transport Archive*

INTO THE 1970s • 83

Seen at the same location, again in the summer of 1972, is ex-'Twin-set' power car No 678; the three trailers that were not permanently fitted to their power cars – No 688-90 – were all withdrawn in 1972. No 678 was to survive in service until 2006 and was preserved on withdrawal. *Philip Hanson/Online Transport Archive*

'Boat' No 603 stands in Rigby Road depot in the autumn of 1972 alongside OMO No 1; the latter was just about to enter service when recorded here and its original livery is in pristine condition. *Marcus Eavis/Online Transport Archive*

84 • THE BLACKPOOL STREAMLINED TRAMS

Having re-entered service barely four months prior to the date of the photograph (17 February 1973), OMO car No 3 heads south from Fleetwood along the reserved track section located between Copse Road and Radcliffe Road at the latter's junction with Stanley Road. No 3 was converted from Series 1 'Railcoach' No 610 (ex-224) with work being completed in October 1972; withdrawn in 1987, the tram was scrapped in June that year. *Alan Murray Rust/Online Transport Archive*

Also recorded on 17 February 1973 is Brush-built No 636 in Talbot Square. Originally No 299, this car has been used a test car following withdrawal in 2009. *Alan Murray-Rust/Online Transport Archive*

Recorded early in 1973, Series 2 'Railcoach' No 614 makes its way southbound along Princes Parade immediately prior to arriving at North Pier. By this stage, No 614 was approaching the end of its life; it was to be withdrawn later in 1973 before being rebuilt as OMO car No 10, which entered service in January 1975. *Philip Hanson/Online Transport Archive*

No 638, still in its all-cream livery, is pictured at Fleetwood Ferry in early 1974 having reverted to normal two-man operation following its unsuccessful period as an OMO car. *Marcus Eavis/Online Transport Archive*

86 • THE BLACKPOOL STREAMLINED TRAMS

When recorded here in early 1974, OMO car No 7 had only recently entered service as it stands at Bispham awaiting departure towards Starr Gate in the company of a 'Balloon' preparing to head for Pleasure Beach. *Marcus Eavis/Online Transport Archive*

Pictured during the summer of 1974, shortly before its withdrawal, No 611 is seen at Starr Gate. Following withdrawal, it was rebuilt as OMO No 12, emerging in this condition in June 1975. Finally withdrawn in 1988 as surplus to requirements, the tram was subsequently scrapped. *Michael H. Waller*

INTO THE 1970s • 87

No 706 heads southbound towards Pleasure Beach having just entered the reserved track section at the south end of Lord Street in Fleetwood during the late spring of 1974. *Marcus Eavis/Online Transport Archive*

During the late spring of 1974 a line-up of five 'Boats' await their next duties in Rigby Road; at the front is No 606. This was to survive in Blackpool until withdrawal in 2000; it was subsequently preserved in the USA. *Marcus Eavis/Online Transport Archive*

Three streamlined cars with No 635 bringing up the rear are seen at Bispham on 14 September 1974. New as No 298 in September 1937, No 635 was approaching the end of its life when recorded here as it was withdrawn later in 1974 and was to be preserved. Acquired by the NTM, it was preserved as – despite its relatively poor condition – it was deemed to have retained more original features than many of the other surviving Brush-built cars. For the next 30 years – until 2005 when the car finally moved to Crich – it was stored at a number of locations with limited restoration work being undertaken. Moved to store in 2014 away from the main Crich site, work on the tram's full restoration – including the construction of a new underframe is scheduled to have commenced by the date of this book's publication. Gerald Druce/Online Transport Archive

INTO THE 1970s • 89

As a sister car makes use of the loop at South Shore, 'Balloon' No 715 heads northbound towards Bispham on 15 September 1974. This tram is still based in Blackpool and is now part of the heritage fleet. Gerald Druce/Online Transport Archive

90 • THE BLACKPOOL STREAMLINED TRAMS

Pictured heading south parallel to Queens Parade, Bispham, with a service towards Starr Gate in September 1974 is No 708. Withdrawn in 2004, No 708 is preserved at the North East Land Sea and Air Museums in Sunderland. *Gerald Druce/Online Transport Archive*

In 1976, No 634 emerged in an overall livery celebrating the centenary of the town; it is seen at Rigby Road towards the end of that year. The special branding was not to last long; No 634 was to emerge the following year with new branding (albeit retaining the wavy blue and yellow colours as illustrated here), this time celebrating the Silver Jubilee of HM Queen Elizabeth II. *Harry Luff/Online Transport Archive*

INTO THE 1970s • 91

Recorded at the Fleetwood terminus in the late spring of 1975 is OMO No 8; by this date, the car in its rebuilt form had been in service for about a year – it had re-entered service in June 1974. One of the handful of OMO cars to survive into 1993, No 8 was preserved on withdrawal. *Harry Luff/Online Transport Archive*

In late 1975, OMO No 7 and No 618 are pictured inside Rigby Road depot alongside a 'Boat'. No 618 was withdrawn in 1975 prior to being rebuilt as OMO No 13 in June 1976. As No 13, it was destined to have a relatively short career, being the first – in 1985 – of the OMO cars to be withdrawn. *Philip Hanson/Online Transport Archive*

92 • THE BLACKPOOL STREAMLINED TRAMS

A contrast in front ends at Fleetwood in late 1975 sees OMO No 5 – by now repainted in the replacement red and cream livery – alongside No 680. By this date, No 680 was operating as single unit with the withdrawal of its associated trailer earlier in the decade. Philip Hanson/Online Transport Archive

Between 1975 and the end of the 1980 season, No 622 wore this striking livery promoting Blackpool Zoo Park. It is seen here approaching the Starr Gate terminus in the early autumn of 1975. Frank Hunt/LRTA (London Area) Collection/Online Transport Archive

INTO THE 1970s • 93

By now resplendent in its replacement red and cream livery, OMO No 3 stands at the Fleetwood Ferry terminus in the early autumn of 1975. Re-entering service in October 1972 following conversion, No 3 was destined to be one of the early OMO cars to be withdrawn, succumbing in 1987 and being scrapped in June of that year. Frank Hunt/LRTA (London Area) Collection/Online Transport Archive

Proof that the summers of the 1970s were not all hot and sunny as 'Balloon' No 707, painted in its overall advert livery promoting Empire Pools is seen heading towards Fleetwood at North Pier on 22 September 1976. Michael H. Waller

94 • THE BLACKPOOL STREAMLINED TRAMS

Standing outside Fleetwood Church at the junction of Adelaide Street and Lord Street, one of the surviving 'Twin car' sets – Nos 682 and 672 – is pictured about to head southbound in the autumn of 1976. This view shows to good effect the conversion of the trailer car to incorporate a driver's cab, a process that was essential once it was decided to operate the majority of the 'Twin car' sets in fixed formations. Harry Luff/Online Transport Archive

By now in the revised red and cream livery, OMO car No 5 heads south towards Starr Gate at Manchester Square on 27 July 1979. The track heading inland at this point, once part of the Lytham Road route, provides access to Rigby Road depot and works.
Les Folkard/Online Transport Archive

INTO THE 1970s • 95

On the same day, OMO car No 11 and Brush-built No 633 pass on South Promenade as they head towards Pleasure Beach and Cabin respectively. *Les Folkard/Online Transport Archive*

A couple of months later, No 633 is pictured again, this time heading towards Starr Gate at the southern end of Lord Street, in Fleetwood, at the point at which the tramway leaves the street and enters the reservation that parallels Lofthouse Way and Radcliffe Road. No 633 remains in Blackpool as part of the heritage fleet. *Marcus Eavis/Online Transport Archive*

96 • THE BLACKPOOL STREAMLINED TRAMS

In 1976, 'Boat' No 603 headed west over the Atlantic to the city of Philadelphia to help mark the bicentenary of American Independence. Four days after the actual anniversary, the car, having been regauged to the Philadelphia gauge of 1,581mm, is seen at 5th Street with, appropriately, Independence Hall in the background. *Edward Springer*

As illustrated earlier, No 634 operated in 1976 wearing a special livery to mark the centenary of the town and, the following year, the livery was modified to celebrate the queen's silver jubilee. Now shorn of the illuminated roof panels that promoted both anniversaries, No 634 is seen here in the early autumn of 1979 in the basic overall livery adopted in 1976. It was to retain this until the start of the 1981 season when the car reappeared in a new overall livery, this time promoting Blackpool Zoo. *Marcus Eavis/Online Transport Archive*

INTO THE 1970s • 97

The same day sees No 718 turn from Pharos Street into North Albert Street having just departed from the Fleetwood Ferry terminus. The loop that acts as the northernmost terminus of the tramway was completed in 1924. As part of the work for the modernisation of the tramway in the twenty-first century, the single track along Pharos Street was segregated and the road made one way. Originally No 255 and new in December 1934, No 718 was to be rebuilt as one of the quartet of 'Millennium' cars in 2002. The Pharos lighthouse was completed in 1840 to the design of Decimus Burton and Captain Henry M. Denham as part of the development of Fleetwood. Linked to a second – shorter – lighthouse on the seafront, it is used to guide shipping across the treacherous sandbanks of the estuary. When recorded in this view, the building's original sandstone had only recently been uncovered; for a number of years it had been painted cream and red. Marcus Eavis/Online Transport Archive

In October 1979, Brush-built No 632 is pictured approaching Bispham with a service towards Fleetwood. This was one of the handful of these trams that was to see service through to the last day of the traditional tramway although it had been sold to the LTT two years earlier. *Alan Murray-Rust/Online Transport Archive*

During the same month, No 709 is pictured departing from Bispham with a southbound service. New in September 1934 as No 246, No 709 was the second tram to be rebuilt as a 'Millennium' tram, with work being completed in 2000. It remains with Blackpool Transport – as do the other three – although their use is now very limited. *Alan Murray-Rust/Online Transport Archive*

INTO THE 1970s • 99

A line-up at Bispham in October 1979 sees No 717 having just arrived at its destination – and about to receive the attention of the bamboo pole in order to reverse the trolley – whilst No 713 departs with a southbound service towards Pleasure Beach. The former remains in Blackpool as part of the heritage fleet whilst the latter, now preserved, is stored in the Blackpool area. *Alan Murray-Rust/Online Transport Archive*

Pictured approaching Bispham from the south in October 1979 is No 708. Withdrawn eventually in 2004, this car is one of a number that are now preserved in Sunderland by the North-East Land, Sea and Air Museums. *Alan Murray-Rust/Online Transport Archive*

THE END OF THE OMO CARS AND DEVELOPMENTS THROUGH TO THE MILLENNIUM

On 22 July 1980, a further collision saw Nos 705 and 706 seriously damaged and, as a result, both cars were withdrawn from service. No 705 was sold for scrap in August 1982 to Lister of Bolton and dismantled in Blundell Street depot two months later. Its trucks, however, were salvaged and were passed over to the Merseyside Transport Preservation Society for use in the restoration of Liverpool No 762 whilst other equipment was retained for the rebuilding of No 706. The restoration of the latter saw the car restored to its original open-top condition – albeit now fitted with a pantograph – with work being completed in time for the tram to reappear for the centenary celebrations in 1985.

In late 1982, 'Balloon' No 701 emerged in a new – predominantly cream – livery whilst, in mid-1984, No 1 appeared in a revised livery of cream with a green waistband, which was eventually to appear on the majority of the OMO cars. The thirteen OMO cars, produced as a stop-gap measure in order to save money, were starting to evince problems; the elongated frames with extended bodies were starting to sag at both ends and authorisation was obtained to purchase a batch of new single-deck cars from East Lancashire Coachbuilders in 1984.

The new cars – destined to become known as the 'Centenary' class – were Nos 641-47 (with the eighth car, No 648, originally being an experimental car, No 651, produced by GEC).

The first of the OMO cars to be withdrawn was the last to have entered service – No 13 – which was to be dismantled on 23 March 1985 after being cannibalised for spares. The plan was that, as the new trams were delivered, so the OMO cars would be taken out of service. This resulted in the withdrawal of Nos 2 and 4 in 1985 and Nos 3, 6, 7 and 9 in 1987. All six, with the exception of No 7 (which was to be used as the basis of No 619, the replica toastrack car, which re-entered service on 14 September 1987), were scrapped. These withdrawals meant that No 12 was the only surviving OMO car in the red and cream livery, with Nos 1, 5, 8 and 11 in the new cream and green livery, whilst No 10 sported an all-over advertising livery.

The plan to see all of the original OMO cars replaced by the new 'Centenary' class was, however, not to be fulfilled. Although there were plans to acquire further examples, these were not progressed and the unreliability of Nos 641-47 in service resulted in the surviving OMO cars remaining in service for longer than anticipated. Nos 1 and 12

THE END OF THE OMO CARS AND DEVELOPMENTS THROUGH TO THE MILLENNIUM • 101

On 18 July 1981, 'Balloon' No 720 stands at the Fleetwood terminus prior to heading back towards Blackpool. As No 257, the tram was originally new in February 1935. Withdrawn in 2006, parts from the tram were used in the restoration of No 717 but refurbishment was to follow. In 2009, the car re-entered service and was the first to be fitted with door pods and power-operated sliding doors. Surviving through to the modernisation of the tramway. No 720 is now one of nine trams derived from the 'Balloon' type to form part of the 'B' fleet in Blackpool, being suitable for operation alongside the new 'Flexity' single-deck cars. *Michael H. Waller*

were withdrawn in 1990, with No 1 being scrapped the following year. Its trucks were salvaged and reused under No 680 whilst No 8 was withdrawn in 1992; No 8 was eventually to be preserved. No 5 was refurbished in 1991 but all three of the remaining cars – Nos 5, 10 and 11 – were withdrawn in 1993. No 5 was preserved on withdrawal and now forms part of the NTM collection. No 10 was acquired in 1996 for use as a café by the Wokefield Park Executive Training & Conference Centre, Reading, after withdrawal; it was scrapped in October 2005. No 11, which departed for Carnforth on 7 July 1993, was converted into a testbed for the experimental 'RoadLiner' No 611 on behalf of Pullman Tram Power Ltd and eventually scrapped in 2000.

Alongside the story of the OMO cars, there were changes to the surviving streamlined cars from the early 1980s onwards. No 638, which had been withdrawn in 1980, was sold for scrap to W. North and disposed of in late 1983. It was replaced in the operational fleet by No 637 which had spent a period acting as the fleet's driver training car.

In 1984, 'Balloon' No 710 was loaned to the National Tramway Museum in place on Glasgow 'Coronation' No 1297 which was moved to Blackpool as one of the cars brought to the town prior to the planned centenary events in 1985.

The Glasgow car was initially to be fitted with a pantograph; although this proved unsuitable – and was quickly replaced by a trolleypole (in place of its existing bow collector) – Blackpool was moving towards adopting the pantograph more widely. In late 1984, 'Balloon' No 712 was fitted with a pantograph constructed by the corporation.

By mid-1985, seven of the OMO cars – Nos 1, 3, 5, 7-10 – plus No 719 and the two modern double-deck cars were also operating with pantographs.

In connection with the centenary, further loans followed: 'Boats' No 600 and 607 were loaned to Heaton Park and the National Tramway Museum respectively. The latter was loaned to permit the return of 'Standard' No 40 to Blackpool. Another 'Boat' to depart Blackpool – this time permanently – was No 603; this had been in store since its return from Philadelphia and was returned to the USA on 19 February 1985 and preserved at El Paso. Both Nos 607 and 710 were returned from Crich to Blackpool at the end of 1985. As part of the plans for the centenary, No 605 was restored to its 1934 condition.

Following its collision with No 705 in 1980, No 706 was stored. It was decided that the car be restored into an open-top condition – similar to that in which it was delivered – for the 1985 centenary. The car, which was restored using parts cannibalised from the scrapped No 705, re-emerged in early 1985. On 6 June 1985, HRH Princess Alice, the Duchess of Gloucester, formally named the car *Princess Alice* in a ceremony held at North Shore.

As a result of the Transport Act of 1985, the tramway passed to new ownership – the corporation-owned Blackpool Transport Services Ltd – in early 1986 and a new general manager – Anthony Depledge – was appointed.

In the late 1980s, five of the Brush-built cars – Nos 621/23/32/34/37 – underwent significant overhauls; this work included the fitting of pantographs and windows from withdrawn OMO cars. No 637 – the last of the quintet to be completed

During the 1970s a series of experiments – with varying degrees of success – were undertaken in the use of pantographs. A number of cars were fitted with pantographs supplied by Brecknell Willis; these included a number of the OMO cars – Nos 4, 5 and 13 – but the trial equipment was subsequently removed. No 5 – seen here during the late summer of 1981 – was the only one of the OMO trio to be refitted with a pantograph, with seven of the type so equipped by the mid-1980s. R.W. A. Jones/Online Transport Archive

THE END OF THE OMO CARS AND DEVELOPMENTS THROUGH TO THE MILLENNIUM • 103

'Twin-car' set No 675 and 685 head south towards Pleasure Beach in the late summer of 1981. Although the tram and trailer look in smart condition, the less that's said about the condition of the traction column the better! In 1975, No 675 had its roof windows panelled over – the only one of the batch to be so treated – and the modified lines of the tram are clearly visible in this view. *R.W.A. Jones/Online Transport Archive*

Recorded at Fleetwood on 26 August 1981 is 'Balloon' No 700; this first of the 'Luxury Dreadnoughts' to be delivered – in February 1934 – the tram remains in Blackpool and now forms part of the tramway's B fleet based at Rigby Road. *John Meredith/Online Transport Archive*

104 • THE BLACKPOOL STREAMLINED TRAMS

A second 'Balloon' – No 707 – is pictured on 26 August 1981, this time on North Albert Street in Fleetwood. This car was eventually the first to be rebuilt as one of quartet of 'Millennium' cars, being completed in 1998. *John Meredith/Online Transport Archive*

A contrast in front ends at North Pier on 26 August 1981 sees 'Balloon' No 718 loading passengers prior to heading northbound to Fleetwood whilst rebuilt No 761 will shortly head north as well with a service to Cleveleys. *John Meredith/Online Transport Archive*

THE END OF THE OMO CARS AND DEVELOPMENTS THROUGH TO THE MILLENNIUM • 105

(in 1990) – underwent the most significant work, including internal repanelling and the introduction of bus seating. The latter proved unpopular and was quickly replaced by alternative bus seating (salvaged from ex-London Transport Routemaster buses which Blackpool had been operating in the post-Deregulation era). Further overhauls of the type followed: No 626 in 1992-94; No 631 in 1995; and No 630 in 1996.

A further loan in the spring of 1988 saw a Blackpool tram visit Scotland for the first time as No 606 headed for Glasgow and use in that year's garden festival; it was to be returned to Blackpool on 25 October 1988.

By 1990, the plastic windscreens fitted to the 'Boats' were starting to show their age, with scratching resulting in reduced visibility for the drivers. As a result, the surviving cars were fitted with replacement two-piece windscreens.

During the summer of 1992, 'Boat' No 602 was fitted with a pantograph; the work involved the fitting of a special canopy to protect the passengers.

A second 'Boat' – No 604 – was similarly fitted the same year. At the same time, No 604 was also fitted with replacement Z6 controllers reused from a withdrawn OMO car in place of its original BTH B18 units; Nos 602 and 605 were also to receive Z6 controllers (the latter in late 1993). No 604 first operated in this guise on 19 July 1992. The same year witnessed the return to service of No 680, initially withdrawn in 1989, following the completion of a £30,000 refurbishment; this work included the replacement of its existing bogies by those from withdrawn OMO car No 1. The use of the pantographs on Nos 602 and 604 was deemed a failure, however, as the special canopies did not prevent grease from dripping on to the passengers; both reverted to conventional trolleypole operation in 1993.

The problem with the pantographs was not the only one to face the 60-year-old 'Boats'; following an inspection in August 1993, which identified faults with the bogies, Nos 602, 604 and 606 were taken out of service whilst No 607, which had had remedial work earlier in the year, and No 605, which had

In July 1982, No 717 passes the church of St Peter's in Fleetwood as it turns from Lord Street into North Albert Street. No 717 remains in Blackpool as part of the heritage fleet. *Alan Murray-Rust/Online Transport Archive*

On the same day No 707 – by now in an overall livery promoting Blackpool's three piers – is recorded in Lord Street heading towards the Fleetwood terminus. There is clearly something slight awry with the car's destination blind! *Alan Murray-Rust/Online Transport Archive*

received the bogies (with Metalastik suspension) from withdrawn a withdrawn OMO car, remained operational. Work on replacing the bogies on the withdrawn trio of 'Boats' was completed in the spring of 1994.

In 1993, No 707 required an overhaul; a number of the 'Balloon' cars had recently undergone work and had emerged largely unchanged – for No 707, however, a considerable rebuild was undertaken. The first evidence of the change was noted in mid-1996, when it was reported that one end had been rebuilt with a smooth end, rounded corners, single-piece windscreen, halogen headlights, larger driver cabs and no side door for access to the cabs. When No 707 emerged in 1998, both ends had been so treated. The revised cab arrangements and improved headlights were designed to improve the driver's visibility, particularly at night on the ill-lit northern section to Fleetwood. Following on from No 707, a further three cars – Nos 709 (in 2000), 718 (in 2002) and 724 (in 2004) – with the quartet becoming known as the 'Millennium' class. Although proving reasonably successful in service, the cars were still expensive to operate as, like the surviving 'Balloon' class, they required a driver and two conductors.

Following an extensive rebuild No 700 emerged at Easter 1997 fully restored to its condition and livery that it carried in 1942. The original twin destination blinds were restored although the tram retained its post-1968 fleet number.

The ranks of the 'Boat' class were further reduced when, on 14 September 2000, No 606 departed for the USA; the car was destined to be swapped to permit the return of 'Standard' No 147 to Blackpool for restoration. Brush-built No 633, which had been stored since January 1999 requiring a major overhaul, was also to be modified; it was to emerge as a new illuminated car – the first for almost four decades – in 2001. This was needed as a result of the withdrawal of the *Rocket* and *Western Train*.

THE END OF THE OMO CARS AND DEVELOPMENTS THROUGH TO THE MILLENNIUM • 107

On 10 August 1982, No 633 heads south past the Lewis's store with a service towards Pleasure Beach followed by one of the OMO cars heading to Starr Gate. No 633 wore the striking red livery promoting the Royal Mail between 1982 and 1984. *Geoffrey Tribe/Online Transport Archive*

Recorded on the Pleasure Beach loop on 18 August 1982 is Brush-built No 627. By this date, the tram had been fitted with the roof-mounted illuminated advertising panels recovered from the withdrawn 'Coronation' class cars. No 627 was finally to be withdrawn in 2004 and was preserved locally. *John Meredith/Online Transport Archive*

108 • THE BLACKPOOL STREAMLINED TRAMS

Recorded in the early summer of 1983 at the Fleetwood terminus in the company of a 'Balloon', No 762 awaits departure with a service to Pleasure Beach. *Harry Luff/Online Transport Archive*

With the loop at Little Bispham occupied by engineering car No 753, OMO No 1 awaits departure with a southbound service to Starr Gate during the spring of 1984 in its third – white and green - livery. Although it had been anticipated that the arrival of the new 'Centenary' class would permit the withdrawal of the OMO cars, problems with the newer trams resulted in a number of the older cars – Nos 1, 5, 8, 10-12 – surviving for longer than anticipated. No 1 was finally withdrawn in 1989 following a compressor fire and accident in Rigby Road. It was scrapped four years later. *Harry Luff/Online Transport Archive*

THE END OF THE OMO CARS AND DEVELOPMENTS THROUGH TO THE MILLENNIUM • 109

Between 1984 and the end of the 1987 season, No 621 operated in a livery promoting the Ice Drome; it is seen here outside Rigby Road depot shortly after the livery was first introduced in the spring of 1984. *R.W.A. Jones/Online Transport Archive*

Another new livery introduced for the 1984 season was that promoting Belles Cuisines on No 626; again seen when newly released, the tram is heading northbound on South Promenade. No 626 retained the livery for two years.
R.W.A. Jones/Online Transport Archive

110 • THE BLACKPOOL STREAMLINED TRAMS

Recorded in the overall advertising livery promoting Little Italy is No 719, seen at Bispham in the spring of 1984. Although still running with a traditional trolleypole here, by the following year, No 719 was fitted with a pantograph. A quarter of a century later, No 719 was to be one of nine 'Balloons' modified in order to operate the second-generation tramway alongside the new 'Flexity' cars as part of the 'B' fleet'. Their use, however, in this guise has been somewhat limited. *R.W.A. Jones/Online Transport Archive*

Following its collision with No 705, No 706 was stored for some four years but it was decided that the car be restored – using parts salvaged from the scrapped No 705 – in open-top condition for the centenary of the tramway in 1985. It first emerged in this condition in early 1985 and is pictured here following its naming as *Princess Alice*. It is seen here with a pantograph; the car has also operated with a traditional trolleypole in this guise as, despite precautions, grease has been known to drip onto unsuspecting passengers. *H. Luff/Online Transport Archive*

THE END OF THE OMO CARS AND DEVELOPMENTS THROUGH TO THE MILLENNIUM • 111

In the period prior to the centenary celebrations of 1985, a number of historic Blackpool trams were loaned back to the corporation from the collection at Crich; in place of 'Standard' No 40, 'Boat' No 607 was loaned to the National Tramway Museum and it seen heading towards Town End during this period. The tram returned to Blackpool later in the year. Ian Stewart/Online Transport Archive

In the late spring of 1985, No 630 stands at Bispham whilst operating a northbound service to Fleetwood. The overall livery promoting Tussauds Waxworks was new for the 1985 season and No 630 would sport it for three years, until the end of the 1987 season. Harry Luff/Online Transport Archive

112 • THE BLACKPOOL STREAMLINED TRAMS

Another tram to appear in a new livery for the 1985 season was No 633; previously this car had operated in a predominantly red livery promoting Royal Mail but, when seen here at North Pier the car had newly re-emerged carrying a livery advertising Kodak film. The tram was to operate in this new livery for four years, until the end of the 1988 season. *Harry Luff/Online Transport Archive*

The conductor looks northwards as No 636 passes the Pleasure Beach loop in the early summer of 1985. The tram is carrying the livery promoting Warburton's that it wore from 1984 until the end of the 1989 season. *R.W.A. Jones/Online Transport Archive*

THE END OF THE OMO CARS AND DEVELOPMENTS THROUGH TO THE MILLENNIUM • 113

Work is in progress on two cars in Rigby Road on 28 September 1985; on the left is No 626, which still shows traces of the Belles Cuisine advertising livery it wore during 1984 and 1985, whilst on the right in OMO Car No 7. No 626 was to emerge the following year bearing a new overall livery, this time promoting the Mighty White loaf. *Harry Luff/Online Transport Archive*

On the same day, No 716 is seen at Norbreck with a northbound service towards Fleetwood. Withdrawn in 2003 as a result of the poor condition of its underframe, No 716 was acquired by the Perth-based Ptarmigan Transport Solutions with a view to conversion into a conference room. However, the business venture failed and No 716 was later to be seen in a scrapyard in Kirkcaldy; it is believed that the tram was subsequently scrapped. *Harry Luff/Online Transport Archive*

114 • THE BLACKPOOL STREAMLINED TRAMS

No 631 draws attention as it heads southbound Little Bispham on 28 September 1985. The tram operated in this livery – promoting Wall's Romero ice cream – for only the 1985 season; it was to re-emerge the following year in a new livery promoting Pricebusters. Harry Luff/Online Transport Archive

Between 1983 and 1985 No 632 operated in the livery promoting Wilson's Brewery; it is seen here towards the end of the period – on 28 September 1985 – at the Metropole. Les Folkard/Online Transport Archive

THE END OF THE OMO CARS AND DEVELOPMENTS THROUGH TO THE MILLENNIUM • 115

Looking in a somewhat careworn condition, OMO No 11 enters the reservation at the southern end of Lord Street on 29 September 1985 with a southbound service towards Starr Gate. Rebuilt from Series 2 'Railcoach' No 615, which had originally been withdrawn in 1974, and re-entering service in November 1975, No 11 was withdrawn finally in 1993. This was not quite to be the end of its story, however, as it was subsequently converted in experimental 'RoadLiner' No 611, a tram that had an intermittent – and not wholly successful – career in Blackpool thereafter. It was finally scrapped in 2000. Alan Murray-Rust/Online Transport Archive

In the early summer of 1988, No 634 is seen at Bispham fitted with a pantograph and in the livery promoting Marton Mere Park that it wore for the three seasons from 1986 to the end of 1988. Harry Luff/Online Transport Archive

116 • THE BLACKPOOL STREAMLINED TRAMS

Also recorded at Bispham during the early summer of 1988 is No 718 in the freshly applied overall livery promoting McDonald's. *Harry Luff/Online Transport Archive*

The Glasgow Garden Festival was held at Plantation Quay, Govan, on the banks of the River Clyde between 26 April and 26 September 1988. Amongst the attractions at the event was a working tramway and amongst the trams featured was 'Boat' No 606, which was to return home late in October. *Geoffrey Tribe/Online Transport Archive*

THE END OF THE OMO CARS AND DEVELOPMENTS THROUGH TO THE MILLENNIUM • 117

In 1989, No 701 underwent a major overhaul; the work undertaken was to set the standard for future overhauls of the type on Nos 711, 719 and 723. The work resulted in a modified appearance. Gone were the curved roof and end windows – the cost of curved glass was prohibitive and getting harder to acquire whilst the use of plastic was not ideal as it weathered badly – whilst the side windows were also replaced by hopper windows. Internally the traditional seating was replaced by fixed units reused from withdrawn Routemaster buses. In keeping with the Routemaster theme, No 701 emerged in the red and white livery then in use on Blackpool Transport's Routemaster buses – acquired from London Transport as a response to bus deregulation – when it re-entered service in 1991. It is seen here standing in front of the North Euston Hotel in Fleetwood shortly after its reappearance. No 701 retained the red and white livery until the end of the 1993 season. *Geoffrey Tribe/Online Transport Archive*

118 • THE BLACKPOOL STREAMLINED TRAMS

On 16 July 1989, No 625 heads south at Copse Road, Fleetwood, with a service towards Starr Gate. This was the last year in which No 625 operated in fleet livery for a period; it reappeared from the 1990 season bearing an overall livery promoting Family Choice, which it carried until the end of the 1992 season. Les Folkard/Online Transport Archive

Following withdrawal as OMO No 7 in early 1987, No 619 was rebuilt as mock crossbench car and emerged in this new condition on 14 September 1987. It operated in a brown, red and white livery reminiscent of the old brown and cream livery adopted by the Blackpool & Fleetwood Tramroad Co between the route's opening on 14 July 1898 and its sale to Blackpool on 1 January 1920 – as seen in this view taken on Ash Street, Fleetwood, on 16 July 1989. Les Folkard/Online Transport Archive

THE END OF THE OMO CARS AND DEVELOPMENTS THROUGH TO THE MILLENNIUM • 119

Recorded on the same day and in the same location is No 607; following withdrawal in 2004, this tram was preserved at the NTM. *Les Folkard/Online Transport Archive*

Two generations of 'Dreadnoughts' stand at Fleetwood Ferry on 16 July 1989; on the left is the sole surviving example from eighteen open-top cars supplied by the Midland Railway Carriage & Wagon Co Ltd in 1900 and 1902 and on the right No 706. The latter had been withdrawn following an accident in 1980 and had originally been slated for scrapping; reprieved, the car was restored to open-top condition and re-entered service in 1985. Modern features such as the lower-deck hopper windows and pantograph were, however, retained. *Les Folkard/Online Transport Archive*

120 • THE BLACKPOOL STREAMLINED TRAMS

Twin set Nos 674 and 684 head north at North Pier on 6 August 1994 with 'Boat' No 605 in the distance. The logo visible on the rear of No 685 was that adopted by Blackpool Transport Services Ltd after the transfer of the assets to the council-owned company as a result of the Transport Act of 1985. *John Meredith/Online Transport Archive*

Seen preparing to head north at the Tower on 6 August is twin set Nos 673 – by now fitted with a pantograph – and 683. The pair were withdrawn in 2010 and subsequently preserved in Fleetwood. *John Meredith/Online Transport Archive*

THE END OF THE OMO CARS AND DEVELOPMENTS THROUGH TO THE MILLENNIUM • 121

No 619 was to remain operational in Blackpool in this guise until final withdrawal in 2009 – although out of service between 2004 and 2008 – and was preserved at Heaton Park. It is seen here at the Tower on 6 August 1994. *John Meredith/Online Transport Archive*

On the same day, one of the surviving 'Boats' – No 606 – is also pictured at the Tower heading southbound towards Pleasure Beach.
John Meredith/Online Transport Archive

122 • THE BLACKPOOL STREAMLINED TRAMS

Between 1992 and 1998 No 637 carried three different versions of liveries promoting Yates's Wine Bar; this view was recorded in 1995. Geoffrey Tribe/Online Transport Archive

No 719, seen here in 1997 (shortly after its conversion), operated as the Wall's Ice Cream tram between 1997 and 2006; this included – for a brief period between 1997 and 1999 – the inclusion of an ice cream counter onboard. This was not, however, deemed a success as the product was more expensive than it was in the adjacent shops. Another problem was that the counter also reduced the seating capacity; this resulted in the tram operating mostly on specials between North Pier and Pleasure Beach until the counter was removed. Geoffrey Tribe/Online Transport Archive

THE END OF THE OMO CARS AND DEVELOPMENTS THROUGH TO THE MILLENNIUM • 123

The first of the quartet of rebuilt 'Balloon' cars No 707 emerged in 1998 and is seen here in July of that year during the weekend that marked the centenary of the opening of the route to Fleetwood. *Philip Hanson/Online Transport Archive*

In 1984, No 600 went to the Heaton Park tramway in Manchester on long-term loan; initially this was to facilitate the transfer of Manchester No 765 to Blackpool so that the latter could feature in the celebrations for the centenary of the Blackpool system in 1985. No 600 was to remain in Manchester until 1998 and is seen here during the summer of that year prior to its return to Blackpool. In order to access the Heaton Park depot, No 600 was modified by the removal of its trolley tower. *Harry Luff/Online Transport Archive*

124 • THE BLACKPOOL STREAMLINED TRAMS

After 1997, No 621 appeared in two versions of a livery promoting Hot Ice – a show held at Blackpool Pleasure Beach – and this view, taken at Fleetwood during 1998, shows the first version of the livery. No 621 was the last of the Brush-built cars to receive the modified new front domes with single destination blind; this process had started in the late 1950s but was not completed until 1980 when No 621 was modified. In the late 1980s, the car was further altered. It received new hopper windows which had been produced specially; unfortunately, the cost involved meant that only No 621 was so equipped so the decision was made to reuse windows from the withdrawn OMO cars instead. No 621 wore the later version of the Hot Ice livery until withdrawn in 2004. *Geoffrey Tribe/Online Transport Archive*

THE END OF THE OMO CARS AND DEVELOPMENTS THROUGH TO THE MILLENNIUM • 125

Largely unchanged structurally since its conversion in the early 1960s, No 678 was a popular tram amongst the enthusiast fraternity. In its later years it wore two liveries supporting the Royal British Legion; this version – recorded in 1998 – was the earlier of the two. No 678 was eventually withdrawn in 2006 and is now preserved in Fleetwood. *Geoffrey Tribe/Online Transport Archive*

Alongside No 678 in its Royal British Legion colours, No 680 was repainted in a livery supporting the Leonard Cheshire homes. It was to carry this livery for six years before it was repainted in a new overall livery promoting Central Pier. Operating for the last time on 30 October 2008 in an all-over blue with yellow chevron livery, No 680 was repainted in cream in September 2010 before being loaned to Beamish for operation in 2014. The car has been based at Heaton Park since March 2015 although is, at the time of writing, back in Blackpool on loan. *Geoffrey Tribe/Online Transport Archive*

126 • THE BLACKPOOL STREAMLINED TRAMS

No 721 in its striking Michelin livery heads north at North Pier with a service towards Thornton Gate in 1998, shortly after an overhaul. No 721 was one of only three of the type – the other two being Nos 700 and 703 – to retain roof windows throughout its operational life. The majority had these windows panelled over during the 1970s and 1980s. The overhaul saw the tram fitted with hopper windows and bus seating on the lower deck, although traditional seating was retained on the upper. The Michelin livery, with its contravision covering the windows, was not popular with passengers as it restricted vision and was subsequently modified. The car retained the basic Michelin livery until 2004. *Geoffrey Tribe/Online Transport Archive*

In the early 1990s a number of the Brush-built cars underwent major refurbishment. The work included replacing the existing windows with examples salvaged from withdrawn OMO cars, the introduction of bus seating, the replacement of the trolleypole with a pantograph and internal repanelling. One of the cars so treated was No 631, which emerged in this revised condition in 1995 and is seen here, some three years later, forming a northbound service on a particularly wet summer's day. The high backs of the bus seats can be seen through the ex-OMO windows. *Philip Hanson/Online Transport Archive*

THE END OF THE OMO CARS AND DEVELOPMENTS THROUGH TO THE MILLENNIUM • 127

Following an extensive overhaul, No 700 re-emerged at the end of March 1997 having been restored close to the livery that it carried during the war and with its twin destination blinds reinstated. It is seen here in July 1998 but with different style lettering on the blinds themselves. *Philip Hanson/Online Transport Archive*

INTO THE MODERN AGE

From the early years of the twenty-first century, the story of the Blackpool system was dominated by the on-off modernisation. That the existing tramway was life-expired was undeniable; decades of make do and mend for both the infrastructure and the vehicles had ensured that the tramway had survived the Millennium but, without significant investment, the future looked bleak. It was suggested that, without upgrading, the system might only survive for a further decade. The scale of the modernisation required was beyond both the company and the local councils to fund, requiring government backing and this took several years (and a number of revised proposals) to achieve.

One facet of the deteriorating condition of the track was the ban on the use of double-deck cars north of Thornton Gate for 18 months from October (it was reversed in April 2004 following track renewal work). One consequence of this was the lack of high capacity trams capable of dealing with the crowds heading for Fleetwood at busy times such as market days. As a result, the surviving twin-car sets operated more regularly to Fleetwood and this was to continue – albeit at a more restricted level – thereafter.

'Boat' No 602 pictured in Rigby Road depot on 15 May 2009 bears the yellow and black 'handy bus' livery in which it was painted in 1990. This livery was similar to the minibus livery adopted by Blackpool Transport at the same time. Following the 2004 season, all of the surviving 'Boats' had been withdrawn in order to reduce the size of the fleet. Following complaints, four of the type – Nos 600/02/04/05 – were reinstated during the 2005 season. No 602 was also withdrawn in 2009 and again reinstated. It was repainted into red and white during 2013 and renumbered to its original pre-1968 number (227) as part of the heritage fleet. Philip Hanson/Online Transport Archive

INTO THE MODERN AGE • 129

Two 'Balloons' – Nos 723 and 726 – allocated to driver training duties are seen in Rigby Road depot on 15 May 2009. The former was withdrawn in 2011, becoming part of the heritage fleet two years later. It was restored to a 1980s livery in 2016. No 726 was withdrawn in 2010 and sold for preservation; it was in open store in Fleetwood but returned – still privately owned – to Rigby Road for further storage, still in its HM Coastguard livery, in 2017. *Philip Hanson/Online Transport Archive*

Whilst the long-term issue of the tramway was under discussion both locally and nationally, the company undertook the refurbishment of the existing fleet. Between 2000 and 2006, six of the surviving 'Balloons' underwent the programme – Nos 713 (2005), 717 (2006), 718 (2002) 719 (2001), 723 (2003) and 724 (2004) – as did the two rebuilt double-deckers – Nos 761 and 762 in 2004 and 2002 respectively – and five of the twin-car sets – Nos 671/81, 672/82, 673/83 and 674/84 in 2003 and 675/85 in 2004. Unrefurbished No 677 was not so lucky, however, as it was last used in 2004 and subsequently stripped for spares with its frames being reused in the rebuild of illuminated car No 733. The associated trailer – No 687 – was used thereafter as a store at Rigby Road prior to being preserved. Also stored at the end of the 2004 season was another unrefurbished twin-car set Nos 676/86.

The end of the 2004 season was to prove a low-water mark for the Blackpool system; a reduction in traffic resulted in no fewer than twenty-five trams being taken out of service. Apart from the 'Twin-car' units already mentioned, all of the surviving Brush-built cars – with the exception of Nos 626, 630 and 631 – were stored, as was 'Balloon' No 722; for five of the Brush cars – Nos 621, 625, 627, 634 and 637 – this was the end of their career (although all still survive in some guise with No 621 now part of the heritage fleet).

130 • THE BLACKPOOL STREAMLINED TRAMS

By 15 May 2009, No 721 was approaching the end of its career when recorded here heading northwards along the Promenade towards the Tower. Withdrawn in November 2009, the tram was sold to the Sunderland-based North East Land, Sea & Air Musuems, where, after a period of outside storage, it is now housed in a custom-built shed. *Philip Hanson/Online Transport Archive*

As part of the programme for the modernisation of the tramway, the section of route between Ash Street and Fleetwood was temporarily closed from November 2009 to enable work to be undertaken. Services were suspended from the end of operation on Sunday 8 November and, over that weekend, a considerable variety of trams ran to mark the end of the traditional tramway. Amongst those in operation on the last night were Nos 673/83 in Metro livery and it is believed that this set was the last of the 'Twin-cars' to work over the Fleetwood street section prior to the suspension. *Philip Hanson/Online Transport Archive*

INTO THE MODERN AGE • 131

Withdrawn in 2003 as a result of defects with its underframe, No 717 was restored to a near original 1930s condition as a result of a substantial bequest received by Blackpool Transport from an enthusiast. The substantial work, which included the construction of a new underframe and stripping back the original body to its framework, took longer to complete than anticipated and the finished car – named *Phillip R. Thorpe* after its benefactor – was not to emerge until the autumn of 2008. It is seen here in July 2010. Although retaining its post-1968 fleet number, the tram has had its traditional twin destination blinds restored. *Philip Hanson/Online Transport Archive*

The upper-deck interior of the restored No 717. Refurbished using parts from a number of other 'Balloons', including Nos 704, 716 and 720, No 717 remains in Blackpool as part of the heritage fleet. *Philip Hanson/Online Transport Archive*

Also withdrawn in late 2004 was No 679; this had been used throughout the year as it had retained its saloon heaters. It was preserved by the LTT in 2006 with the intention that it was restored to its original streamlined condition for the 125th anniversary celebrations in 2010. However, with work incomplete, it was passed back to Blackpool Transport for eventual restoration as part of the heritage fleet.

Three of the Brush-built cars – Nos 626, 630 and 631 – started the 2005 season; these were eventually supplemented by Nos 622 and 623 although the latter spent most of year in use on driver training duties. The following year saw No 622, 626, 630 and 631 in operation but No 624 was sold for preservation; the latter finally left Rigby Road in 2009. No 636 departed Blackpool to be used as a test-bed by Derby-based Stored Energy Technology; it was to return to Blackpool for testing before being finally sold to the company in 2009. It remains in Derby at the time of writing. Also withdrawn in 2006 was No 678; this, unlike Nos 679 and 680, had not undergone major overhaul during 1989 and 1990. As a result, its body condition was poor and an internal swamping due to heavy rain led to its withdrawal. It was preserved locally.

Although No 722 had been stored at the end of the 2004 season, it was restored to service in July the following year. Two years later, however, in October 2007, it was involved in a collision with No 711 and suffered serious damage to its underframe. Again withdrawn, the car war used as a source of spares and as a test-bed for the installation of the power-operated doors that were to be fitted to those 'Balloons' destined to operate alongside the new 'Flexity' cars. With this work completed, No 722 was scrapped in October 2009 – only the second of the type to suffer that fate (the other being No 705 in October 1982) up until that date.

Also in 2007, No 623 briefly reappeared in service; it had been restored to its wartime livery and meant that five of the type – Nos 622/23/26/30/31 – were in use during that year. By 2009, with Nos 622 and 626 withdrawn,

'Balloon' No 719 – now shorn of its Wall's ice cream identity – heads southbound through Talbot Square during the summer of 2010. Shortly after the date of the photograph, No 719 entered Rigby Road to be upgraded to work alongside the new 'Flexity' trams, re-entering service in 2012. *Philip Hanson/Online Transport Archive*

INTO THE MODERN AGE • 133

only two of the type – Nos 630 and 631 – were in service by the end of the year and, with the modernisation progressing, the remaining Brush cars were all offered for sale early in 2010 for transfer once the new system was operational. No 632 was sold to the LTT at the end of 2009 but was used in service during 2010 and 2011 prior to the introduction of the 'Flexity' trams. No 622 was sold as a source of spare parts to the LTT and its body was subsequently converted into a classroom at Anchorsholme Primary School in 2014 (where it remains at the time of writing). Three of the type – Nos 630-32 – were operational towards the end of the conventional tramway with Nos 631 and 632 surviving through to the very end. No 630 was repainted shortly before the conversion into its livery from the 1990s prior to its transfer to the National Tramway Museum. The last of the three surviving 'Twin-set' power cars that had lost their trailers in the early 1970s to survive – No 680 – was also taken out of service at the end of 2009. Acquired by the Heaton Park Tramway, the car remained at Blackpool until 2014 and then spent a year at Beamish before arriving in Manchester.

The same year witnessed the final demise of the replica 'Toastrack' car No 619; it was transferred on loan to Heaton Park in exchange for Manchester No 765, which was required for the 125th anniversary in 2010, and, although the Manchester car has returned home, No 619 remains at Heaton Park.

Amongst the older cars that survived into the modernised era were the four 'Millennium' class cars – Nos 707, 709, 718 and 724 – but, despite have power-operated doors (similar to the refurbished 'Balloons'), these have not operated in service since 2013. They remain in store, however, at Rigby Road.

Following overhaul during the winter of 2002 and 2003, two of the 'Twin-car' sets were taken into Rigby Road depot for overhaul; following the work, the two sets emerged wearing the new Metro livery. Nos 671/81 appeared wearing Line 2 branding whilst Nos 672/82 – seen here during the 125th celebrations in September 2010 – received the Line 1 branding. Although Nos 671/81 were withdrawn in 2009, Nos 672/82 were to operate on the last day of the conventional tramway in 2011 and have been subsequently restored to their original 1960s livery of all-cream with their pre-1968 fleet numbers (Nos 272 and T2) shown. *Philip Hanson/Online Transport Archive*

134 • THE BLACKPOOL STREAMLINED TRAMS

In 1971, No 624 was converted into a works car No 259; it was subsequently renumbered 748. Seen here during 2010 in Rigby Road depot in its overall green livery as adopted in 1971 and still showing evidence of its 1971 number, the tram was subsequently loaned to the LTT and stored in the open at Burton Road before returning to Blackpool Transport in 2014. Philip Hanson/Online Transport Archive

Of the surviving 'Twin-car' sets, two – Nos 671/81 and 674/84 – were withdrawn at the end of 2009 and Nos 673/83 followed in 2010 along with Nos 671/81, which had been temporarily reprieved to supplement the surviving cars for that year's illuminations. This left Nos 672/82 and 675/85 still in service on the last day of the conventional tramway in 2011. No 672/82 was eventually retained as part of the heritage fleet and the cars have now reverted to their original pre-1968 identities as Nos 272 and T2. Nos 675/85 are also part of the heritage fleet, having been restored to their 1970s condition in 2015.

As the end of the conventional tramway grew closer, so the number of 'Balloon' cars was reduced. No 703 was withdrawn in 2009 and sold to the North of England Museum at Beamish where it was restored in Sunderland livery (operating for a period as No 101). Later the same year No 722 was scrapped; it had been withdrawn the previous year and had been a source of spare parts in order to maintain the operation of the remaining cars. Three of the type were preserved in 2010: No 702 passed to the Heaton Park Tramway (eventually); No 712 headed for the National Tramway Museum; and, No 721 was

'Balloon' No 715 was one of a number of the type painted into Metro livery during 2008; it emerged in light blue and yellow. Others so treated that year were Nos 711 (green and yellow) and 713 (purple and yellow). These followed No 710, which had emerged in a yellow and purple Metro livery earlier in the decade. No 715 is seen in Rigby Road during September 2010. *Philip Hanson/Online Transport Archive*

From 1998 No 630 operated in various liveries promoting Go-Karting 2000; it is seen here at Ash Street, Fleetwood, on 24 September 2010 wearing the final version of the livery. One of three of the Brush-built cars to see service in 2011, No 630 was withdrawn shortly before the end of the conventional tramway in order to be repainted in green and cream livery the type carried in the 1990s. It was transferred to the NTM in early 2012. *Les Folkard/Online Transport Archive*

On the same day, one of the quartet of 'Millennium' trams – No 724 – is seen outside the Metropole with a southbound service heading towards Pleasure Beach. *Les Folkard/Online Transport Archive*

INTO THE MODERN AGE • 137

On 25 September 2010 No 604 stands at North Pier; at the time of writing it is renumbered back to its pre-1968 identity of No 230 and named *George Formby OBE*, this is one of three 'Boats' that survive as part of Blackpool's heritage fleet, although at the time of writing it is currently out of service awaiting an overhaul. Les Folkard/Online Transport Archive

Sold to the LTT for preservation in 2009, No 632 was, however, to see operation in both 2010 and 2011. Before the start of the 2010 season, it received the recently refurbished trucks from No 622 (which had been sold to the LTT as a source of spares) and re-entered service in June 2010 having been repainted into the half cream/half green livery in which it is seen here at North Pier on 26 September 2010. One of the Brush-built cars in use on the final day of the conventional tramway – 6 November 2011 – No 632 spent some time in open storage prior to returning to Rigby Road in mid-2014. Les Folkard/Online Transport Archive

No 700 – seen here in August 2012 – was one of only three 'Balloons' to retain their roof windows throughout their operational career; the others were Nos 703 and 721. Towards the end of the twentieth century, it had been restored back to a near original condition although, following a number of accidents, the trolleypole with which it had been fitted was replaced by a pantograph in 2005. Although it had reverted to a more historic form – including the twin destination blinds – the car was one of those selected to be modified to enable operation alongside the new tramcars then being planned for. The work included the installation of power-operated doors and the reuse of bus seats salvaged from No 721 on the lower deck. No 700 was to emerge in this new condition – allied to the purple and white livery illustrated here – during 2009. As such, the tram forms part of the 'B' fleet although sees relatively little use. Philip Hanson/Online Transport Archive

acquired by the Sunderland-based North-East Land, Sea and Air Museums. Another departure in 2010 was No 716; this was acquired by a Scottish-based company with the intention of using the tram as a conference facility. This failed and No 716 was subsequently scrapped.

In order to be able to use the raised platforms constructed for the new generation of 'Flexity' trams, a number of the 'Balloons' scheduled to form part of the 'B' fleet – designed to supplement the modern trams – received power-operated doors. These were Nos 700/07/09/11/13/18-20/24; however, their use has been limited as the modern trams – allied to the growing heritage fleet – have been capable of handling most of the traffic.

Three further 'Balloons' were withdrawn at the end of the 2010 season: Nos 701, 715, and 726 – No 701 becoming part of the heritage fleet, No 715 being acquired by the LTT (and later to return as part of the heritage fleet) and No 726 being preserved locally. The following year No 723 was withdrawn; it too eventually passed to the heritage fleet.

ILLUMINATED TRAMS

One of the features of Blackpool is the town's annual illuminations; over the years, the corporation supplemented the annual display of lighting along the promenade with the operation of special illuminated trams. By the late 1950s, the existing illuminated cars were increasingly life-expired and the corporation used a number of withdrawn trams as the basis of replacement illuminated cars from 1959 onwards. Although the older 'Pantograph' type was also used, two of the Series 1 'Railcoaches' were converted: in 1962 No 209 was used as the basis for the construction of the 'Santa Fe' locomotive, whilst in 1963, No 222 became the 'Hovertram'.

By the late 1950s, the existing illuminated trams were becoming life-expired and, with the reduction in the fleet that resulted from the closures of the period from 1961 to 1963, the opportunity was taken to convert a number of withdrawn trams into new illuminated cars. In 1962, Series 1 'Railcoach' No 209 was used as the basis of the Western locomotive, with 'Pantograph' No 174 being used for the carriage. The new set is seen here when relatively new when sponsored by ABC television. *Harry Luff/Online Transport Archive*

140 • THE BLACKPOOL STREAMLINED TRAMS

More recently, in 2001, one of the surviving ex-Brush built 'Railcoaches' – No 633 was to be converted into the Fisherman's Friend Trawler.

Under the 1968 renumbering scheme, the locomotive became No 733 and the 'Hovertram' No 735. Following its conversion, No 633 was eventually to become No 737. No 733 remained in service until 1999 when it and its associated trailer – No 734 converted from 'Pantograph' car No 174 – were withdrawn as they both needed rewiring and there was evidence that the frames of No 733 were failing. Stored in Rigby Road thereafter, apart from one brief public appearance in 2003, it was not until 2007 that it was announced that the cars were to be restored, funded in part by the Heritage Lottery Fund. A new frame for No 733 was constructed, utilising in part the frames from scrapped twin-set power car No 677. The set returned to service in 2009.

No 735 was withdrawn in 2001, again in need of a rewire and major overhaul, and was sold for preservation in 2007. Initially, it was displayed at the Beith Bus Museum in Ayrshire. It was to reside in Scotland for seven years before transfer to the North-East Land, Sea & Air Museums in Sunderland – where it renewed acquaintance with a number of other ex-Blackpool trams on display there – before returning to Rigby Road two years later; it remains in store there.

Recorded on 15 May 2009 is the illuminated Western Train. This was initially created in 1962, however, by the first decade of the twenty-first century, the underframe of the locomotive was starting to show its age and, following the scrapping of No 677 in June 2007, the underframe and part of the body from the scrapped tram were used to refurbish the locomotive. *Philip Hanson/Online Transport Archive*

ILLUMINATED TRAMS • 141

On the 14th of November 1981, the 'Hovertram' – No 735 – and preserved Bolton No 66 were used on a tour; the pair are seen here at Thornton Gate. At the time, the Hovertram was sponsored by the locally-based estate agents owned by Owen Oyston; prior to the company's sale to Royal Insurance for a reported £37 million, Oyston's was the country's largest family-owned estate agency. Following the sale, Oyston took over Blackpool FC; this led eventually to legal problems and local controversy with fans boycotting the club. The 'Hovertram' was converted from withdrawn Series 1 'Railcoach' No 222 in 1963. Withdrawn in 2001 and sold into preservation six years later, the tram was eventually to be returned to Blackpool where, at the time of writing, it remains in store in Rigby Road depot. *Alan Murray-Rust/Online Transport Archive*

142 • THE BLACKPOOL STREAMLINED TRAMS

The most recent of Blackpool's streamlined cars is No 737, which was converted from No 633 in 2001. The *Fisherman's Friend Trawler* is seen here in November 2011 whilst operating one of the Illuminations Tours. *M. J. Russell*

Following the close of the BR line between Havant and Hayling Island, there were efforts to see the branch preserved. The Hayling Light Railway Society acquired Blackpool No 11 for possible use and the tram is seen here in the goods yard at Havant on 23 October 1965. Following the failure of the preservation scheme, the future of No 11 was secured when it was transferred to the new East Anglian Transport Museum, where it remains.
John Meredith/Online Transport Archive

ILLUMINATED TRAMS • 143

The first 'Boat' to be preserved in the USA was No 601, which was sold in 1971 to the Western Railway Museum, Suisin City, California, where it remains now renumbered to its original pre-1968 fleet number. When it first arrived in California during October 1971, it was initially intended that the tram be operated on the Muni system as part of the San Francisco British Week but, unfortunately a dockyard strike prevented it being unloaded in time and so it went directly to the museum. However, it was to see service – as illustrated here – in San Francisco during September 1983 as part of the city's Trolley Festival. *Harry Luff Collection/Online Transport Archive*

In 1976, No 603 was loaned to Philadelphia as part of the bicentenary celebrations for the USA; regauged for operation on the 1,581mm gauge system of SEPTA, the tram returned to Blackpool two years later but never re-entered service. In 1984, the tram made a further – and at the time of writing final – crossing of the Atlantic when it was sold to the San Francisco Municipal Railway (Muni) for use on one of that operator's heritage tram routes (F Market and Wharves). It is seen here on 26 April 1992 during an anniversary parade. *Harry Luff Collection/Online Transport Archive*

144 • THE BLACKPOOL STREAMLINED TRAMS

Recorded in April 1973, 'VAMBAC' No 11 is 'work in progress' at the East Anglian Transport Museum at Carlton Colville. Michael H. Waller

Following its final withdrawal in 2009, the unique replica crossbench car was preserved at Heaton Park, where it is pictured in service the following year.
Phil Hanson/Online Transport Archive

PRESERVATION

The first of the streamlined trams to be preserved was Marton 'VAMBAC' No 11; withdrawn with the other surviving cars from the batch when the Marton service was converted to bus operation in October 1962, No 11 was initially preserved as part of a putative scheme to preserved the closed Hayling Island railway branch. Following the failure of that scheme, the car was transferred to the East Anglian Transport Museum at Carlton Colville.

The National Tramway Museum is host to six surviving cars. These are 'Boat' No 236, Brush-built No 630 (ex-293) of 1937 and sister car No 298 (which is currently in store at Clay Cross in a partially restored condition; the intention being ultimately to see the tram restored to its original condition). Also in store at Clay Cross is one of the two surviving one-man cars, No 5. Acquired in 2010 following its withdrawal in Blackpool is 'Balloon' No 712; prior to transfer to Crich for display, the tram was overhauled in Blackpool and renumbered 249. Although retaining its wartime top cover, No 249 now displays the livery that the 'Balloons' wore when new in the 1930s. The final one of this sextet is the unique double-deck No 762, which was rebuilt from 'Balloon' No 714.

There are also five cars based on the Heaton Park Tramway. These include two of the 'Balloons' – No 702 at the tramway itself and No 708 in store at Rigby Road – and Brush-built No 623 of 1937.

The other two are the 1987-built toastrack car No 619, which was constructed from OMO No 7 (itself rebuilt earlier from the much modified No 619) and twin-set power car No 680; the latter is on loan to Blackpool Transport and based at Rigby Road.

Based at the North Eastern Electrical Transport Trust, part of the North-East Land, Sea & Air Museums at Sunderland are a further three cars. These comprise 'Balloon' No 721 and a full twin-set Nos 674 and 684.

Closer to Blackpool, the Fleetwood Heritage Leisure Trust possesses seven cars, of these Brush-built No 290 is currently stored at Rigby Road whilst the others are based at Fleetwood but with no public access. These six are Brush-built No 637, 'Balloon' No 710, twin-set Nos 673 and 683, twin-set power car No 678 and trailer No 687.

Apart from the trams housed at Rigby Road as part of the heritage fleet of the Blackpool Heritage Trust and those detailed above, there are a number of privately preserved trams based at their traditional home. These include 'Balloon' No 726 and Brush-built No 625.

No fewer than four of the 'Boats' are preserved in the USA; these are Nos 601 (Western Railway Museum, Suisun City, California), 603 and 605 (both with San Francisco Municipal Transportation Authority) and 606 (at the National Capital Trolley Museum in Washington).

APPENDICES

APPENDIX 1 – BASIC DATA

Number	New	Bodies	Bogies	Seats	Controllers	Motors
200	1933	EE	EE 4ft 0in	50[1]	EE DB1 Z4	EE 305A
201-24	1933/34	EE	EE 4ft 0in	50[1]	EE DB1 Z4	EE 305A
225-36	1934	EE	EE 4ft 0in	56	EE DB1 K44E (225 and 226 [ii]); BTH B18 (227-36)[2]	EE DK34 (225 and 226 (ii); EE27A (227-36)
237 (ex-226 [i])	1934	EE	EE 4ft 9in	94	E DB1 K44	EE DK34B[3]
238-49	1934	EE	EE 4ft 9in	94	EE DB1 Z6	EE 305E
250-63	1934/35	EE	EE 4ft 9in	84[4]	EE DB1 Z6	EE 305E
264-83	1935	EE	EE 4ft 0in	48[5]	EE DB1 Z6	EE 305E
284-303	1937	Brush	EMB Hornless 4ft 3in	50[1]	Allen West CTJ[6]	CP C162[7]
10-21	1939	EE	EE[8]	56[9]	EE DB1 K53E[10]	BTH 265C[11]
T1-T10	1960/61	MCW	M&T	66[12]	n/a	n/a

NOTES:
1. Later reduced to 48 with removal of two folding seats on centre platform.
2. In 1951 Nos 225 and 226 had replacement K53E controllers reused from 'Sun Saloons' as did No 236 in 1959.
3. This was motor when new; soon replaced by EE 305E.
4. Reseated to 94 seats in 1960/61 (Nos 253/55/56) and 1967 (No 258).
5. Nos 272-81 rebuilt for use with trailers; Nos 272-77/81 revised to 53 seats in 1963/64 when permanently couples to Nos T1-T7.
6. Replaced with EE 305A ex-Nos 200-24 between 1963 and 1967.
7. Replaced with EE Z4 ex-Nos 200-24 between 1963 and 1967.
8. Received replacement M&T HS44 bogies between 1949 and 1952.
9. Reduced to 48 between 1948 and 1951.
10. Received replacement VAMBAC equipment between 1949 and 1952.
11. Received replacement CP C92 between 1949 and 1952.
12. Seating reduced to 61 on Nos T1-T7 when fitted with one EE Z6 controller for working fixed to Nos 281 and 272-77 respectively.

APPENDIX 2 – INDIVIDUAL TRAM HISTORY

Number	New	1968 number	Withdrawn	Fate
200	June 1933	—	1962	Scrapped March 1963 (Marton)
201	December 1933	—	1963	Scrapped 27 September 1963 (Thornton Gate)
202	December 1933	—	1963	Scrapped 31 August 1963 (Thornton Gate)
203	January 1934	—	1962	Scrapped December 1962 (Rigby Road)
204	January 1934	—	1962	Scrapped 30 October 1963 (Thornton Gate)
205	January 1934	—	1962	Scrapped July 1963 (Rigby Road)
206	January 1934	—	1961	Scrapped 22 September 1961 (Bispham)
207	January 1934	—	1962	Scrapped March 1963 (Marton)
208	January 1934	—	1962	Scrapped March 1963 (Marton)
209	January 1934	—	1962	Frames/trucks to 733
210	January 1934	—	1962	Scrapped March 1963 (Marton)
211	January 1934	—	1965	Scrapped June 1965 (Bispham)
212	January 1934	—	1965	Scrapped June 1965 (Bispham)
213	January 1934	—	1965	Scrapped June 1965 (Bispham)
214	January 1934	—	1962	Scrapped March 1963 (Marton)
215	January 1934	—	1963	Scrapped 6 November 1963 (Thornton Gate)
216	February 1934	—	1965	Scrapped June 1965 (Bispham)
217	February 1934	—	1965	Scrapped June 1965 (Bispham)
218	February 1934	—	1963	Scrapped 19 September 1963 (Thornton Gate)
219	February 1934	—	1962	Scrapped July 1963 (Rigby Road)
220	February 1934	[608]*	1963	Stored until 1972 then rebuilt as OMO No 4
221	February 1934	[609]*	1965	PWD No 5 from 21 April 1965 then rebuilt as OMO No 5 in 1972
222	February 1934	—	1963	Frames/trucks to No 735
223	February 1934	—	1962	Scrapped March 1963 (Marton)
224	May 1934	610	1969	Used as PW car between October 1964 and May 1965; rebuilt as OMO No 3 in 1972
225	February 1934	600	In service	Part of the Blackpool heritage fleet; named *Duchess of Cornwall*
226 (i)	February 1934	—	—	Renumbered 237 August 1934; see below
226 (ii)	August 1934	601	1970	Preserved (USA)
227	July 1934	602	In service	Part of the Blackpool heritage fleet; named *Charlie Cairoli*
228	July 1934	603	1975	Preserved (USA)
229	July 1934	—	1963	Scrapped April 1968 (Blundell Street)
230	August 1934	604	In service	Part of the Blackpool heritage fleet
231	August 1934	—	1963	Scrapped April 1968 (Blundell Street)
232	August 1934	—	1963	Scrapped April 1968 (Blundell Street)
233	August 1934	605	uncertain	Preserved (USA)
234	August 1934	—	1963	Scrapped April 1968 (Blundell Street)
235	August 1934	606	September 2000	Preserved (USA)
236	August 1934	607	July 2004	Preserved (NTM)
237	February 1934	700	In service	Blackpool B fleet
238	September 1934	701	In service	Part of the Blackpool heritage fleet
239	September 1934	702	2009	Preserved (Heaton Park)

Number	New	1968 number	Withdrawn	Fate
240	September 1934	703	Stored	Part of the Blackpool heritage fleet; preserved at Beamish between withdrawal and 2017
241	September 1934	704	2003	Stored (Blackpool); restoration project announced March 2019 that will see it revert to No 241 in early fully-enclosed state
242	September 1934	705	July 1980	Scrapped October 1982
243	September 1934	706	Stored	Withdrawn following an accident in July 1980 and restored to open-top condition and to service 1985; part of Blackpool heritage fleet
244	September 1934	707	n/a	Rebuilt 1998 as Millennium car
245	September 1934	708	November 2004	Part of Blackpool heritage fleet; previously preserved elsewhere
246	September 1934	709	n/a	Rebuilt 2000 as Millennium car
247	October 1934	710	April 2007	Preserved in open storage at Fleetwood
248	October 1934	711	In service	Blackpool B fleet
249	October 1934	712	November 2009	Preserved (NTM)
250	December 1934	713	In service	Blackpool B fleet
251	December 1934	714	1972	Rebuilt as No 762
252	January 1935	715	In service	Part of the Blackpool heritage fleet
253	February 1935	716	2003	Sold to Scottish buyer 2010; later to scrap yard at Kirkcaldy. Believed to have been scrapped.
254	December 1934	717	In service	Part of the Blackpool heritage fleet
255	December 1934	718	n/a	Rebuilt 2002 as Millennium car
256	February 1935	719	In service	Blackpool B fleet; named *Donna's Dream House*
257	February 1935	720	Stored	Blackpool B fleet
258	March 1935	721	October 2009	Preserved (Sunderland)
259	February 1935	722	2007	Scrapped October 2009
260	January 1935	723	In service	Part of the Blackpool heritage fleet
261	February 1935	724	n/a	Rebuilt 2004 as Millennium car
262	January 1935	725	1971	Rebuilt as No 761
263	February 1935	726	November 2010	Part of the Blackpool heritage fleet
264	June 1935	611	1974	Rebuilt as OMO No 12
265	June 1935	612	1972	Rebuilt as OMO No 8
266	June 1935	613	1973	Rebuilt as OMO No 9
267	June 1935	614	1973	Rebuilt as OMO No 10
268	June 1935	615	1974	Rebuilt as OMO No 11
269	July 1935	616	1970	Rebuilt as OMO No 1
270	July 1935	617	1972	Rebuilt as OMO No 6
271	July 1935	618	1975	Rebuilt as OMO No 13
272	July 1935	672	—	Rebuilt September 1960
273	July 1935	673	—	Rebuilt June 1961
274	July 1935	674	—	Rebuilt May 1962
275	July 1935	675	—	Rebuilt April 1958
276	July 1935	676	—	Rebuilt April 1958
277	July 1935	677	—	Rebuilt July 1960
278	July 1935	678	—	Rebuilt September 1961
279	July 1935	679	—	Rebuilt April 1961

280	July 1935	680	—	Rebuilt December 1960
281	July 1935	671	—	Rebuilt November 1960
282	August 1935	619	1972	Rebuilt as OMO No 7
283	September 1935	620	1970	Rebuilt as OMO No 2
284	July 1937	621	November 2004	Part of the Blackpool heritage fleet
285	July 1937	622	2009	Extant; used as a classroom at Anchorsholme Primary School
286	July 1937	623	2009	Preserved (Heaton Park)
287	July 1937	624	1971	To PWD No 259 (subsequently renumbered 748); withdrawn 2003; donated to LTT for restoration but subsequently returned to Blackpool Transport in 2014
288	July 1937	625	November 2004	Part of the Blackpool heritage fleet
289	August 1937	626	2010	Preserved (Birkenhead)
290	August 1937	627	November 2004	Part of the Blackpool heritage fleet
291	August 1937	628	1969	To PWD No 751; currently in store
292	August 1937	629	1972	Scrapped November 1972
293	August 1937	630	October 2011	Preserved (NTM)
294	August 1937	631	2011	Part of the Blackpool heritage fleet
295	August 1937	632	2011	Preserved (Blackpool)
296	August 1937	633	1997	Rebuilt 2001 as illuminated trawler (No 737)
297	August 1937	634	2004	Preserved (Blackpool)
298	September 1937	635	1974	Preserved (NTM)
299	September 1937	636	2004	Extant (used as a test tram at Derby)
300	September 1937	637	September 2004	Withdrawn 1982; reinstated 1985. Preserved in open storage at Fleetwood
301	September 1937	—	1966	Scrapped April 1968
302	October 1937	638	1980	Scrapped 1983
303	October 1937	—	1962	Scrapped March 1963
10	August 1939	—	1958	Scrapped 15 February 1961 (Rigby Road)
11	August 1939	—	1962	Preserved (EATM)
12	August 1939	—	1962	Scrapped March 1963 (Marton)
13	August 1939	—	1962	Scrapped March 1963 (Marton)
14	August 1939	—	1961	Used as a driver training car after withdrawal and scrapped March 1963 (Marton)
15	August 1939	—	1962	Scrapped March 1963 (Marton)
16	September 1939	—	1962	Scrapped March 1963 (Marton)
17	September 1939	—	1962	Scrapped March 1963 (Marton)
18	October 1939	—	1962	Scrapped March 1963 (Marton)
19	October 1939	—	1962	Scrapped March 1963 (Marton)
20	October 1939	—	1962	Scrapped March 1963 (Marton)
21	October 1939	—	1961	Withdrawn for spares ; scrapped January 1962 (Marton)

* Number allocated but never carried.

Rebuilt cars

281	November 1960	671	November 2010	Part of the Blackpool heritage fleet
272	September 1960	672	Stored	Part of the Blackpool heritage fleet
273	June 1961	673	October 2010	Preserved in open storage at Fleetwood
274	May 1962	674	2008	Preserved (Sunderland)

Number	New	1968 number	Withdrawn	Fate
275	April 1958	675	In service	Part of the Blackpool heritage fleet
276	April 1958	676	2004	Part of the Blackpool heritage fleet
277	July 1960	677	2004	Parts used 2007 to restore *Western* locomotive (No 733)
278	September 1961	678	October 2006	Preserved in open storage at Fleetwood
279	April 1961	679	2004	Preserved; being restored to original condition
280	December 1960	680	2009	Preserved (Heaton Park on loan to Blackpool)
Trailer cars				
T1	July 1960	681	November 2010	Part of the Blackpool heritage fleet
T2	August 1960	682	Stored	Part of Blackpool heritage fleet
T3	September 1960	683	October 2010	Preserved in open storage at Fleetwood
T4	1960	684	2008	Preserved (Sunderland)
T5	1960	685	In service	Part of Blackpool heritage fleet
T6	1960	686	2004	Part of the Blackpool heritage fleet
T7	1960	687	2004	Preserved in open storage at Fleetwood
T8	1960	688	1972	Scrapped
T9	1960	689	1972	Scrapped summer 1989
T10	January 1961	690	1972	Scrapped summer 1989
OMO Cars				
1	October 1972		June 1989	Scrapped November 1993
2	October 1972		February 1985	Scrapped January 1987
3	October 1972		January 1987	Scrapped June 1987
4	October 1972		March 1985	Scrapped January 1987
5	November 1972		March 1993	Preserved (NTM)
6	April 1973		September 1987	Scrapped July 1988
7	July 1973		February 1987	Rebuilt as No 619 (see below)
8	June 1974		May 1992	Preserved (Blackpool)
9	December 1974		July 1987	Scrapped July 1988
10	January 1975		November 1992	Used from 1996 as a café at Wokefield Park Executive Training & Conference Centre, Reading, after withdrawal; scrapped October 2005
11	November 1975		March 1993	Converted as a testbed for experimental RoadLiner No 611 and scrapped 2000
12	November 1975		September 1988	Scrapped October 1993
13	June 1976		June 1984	Scrapped March 1985
761	July 1979		November 2011	Preserved (Blackpool)
762	April 1982		November 2011	Preserved (NTM)
Replica Crossbench car				
619	August 1987		2009	Withdrawn 2004; reinstated 2008; preserved (Heaton Park)
Millennium cars				
707	1998		In service	Blackpool B fleet
709	2000		Stored	Blackpool B fleet
718	2002		In service	Blackpool B fleet
724	2004		Stored	Blackpool B fleet

BIBLIOGRAPHY

Bett, W. H. and Gillham, J. C.; edited by Price, J. H, *The Tramways of North Lancashire*; LRTA; undated

Johnson, Peter; *Trams in Blackpool*; AB Publishing; 1986

Meskell, Nick; *Blackpool Trams 1950-1967*; Train Crazy Publishing; 2019

Modern Tramway/Tramways & Urban Transit; LRTA; 1937 onwards

Palmer, Steve, *A Nostalgic Look at Blackpool Trams 1950-1966*; Silver Link; 1995

Palmer, Steve, and Turner, Brian, *Blackpool by Tram*; published by the authors in association with the Transport Publishing Co; third edition; 1981

Palmer, Steve, *Blackpool's Centenary of Trams*; Blackpool Borough Council Transport Department; 1985

Tramtrax

Waller, Peter, *Regional Tramways: The North West of England post 1945*; Pen & Sword; 2017

Waller, Peter, *The Classic Trams: 30 Years of Tramcar Design 1920-1950*; Ian Allan Publishing; 1993